# Grow *with* Joe

## *by* JOE MAIDEN

GREAT NORTHERN

Grow*with*Joe

Great Northern Books
PO Box 213, Ilkley, LS29 9WS
www.greatnorthernbooks.co.uk

First published 2010.
Reprinted 2010.

ISBN: 978 1 905080 79 3

Design and layout: David Burrill

CIP Data
A catalogue for this book is available from the British Library

# CONTENTS

The old potting shed, from where Joe Maiden co-presents *Tim and Joe* on BBC Radio Leeds every Sunday morning.

Joe inside the potting shed – and ready to broadcast.

# FOREWORD

## by Tim Crowther

Being invited to write this foreword is a true honour, for which I thank one of life's true gents, Mr Joseph Reeder Maiden.

Joe has been my mate ever since some bright spark producer invited us to present a gardening programme together on BBC Radio Leeds. That was more than fifteen years ago, and because of Joe's enthusiasm, humour, ability to communicate and endless knowledge of horticulture, the programme has developed a life of its own. It's a weekly ratings topper, of which we are both very proud. That said, quite what my role is or qualities are remain a mystery, not least to me – but we do seem to work together very well.

You see, over the course of three hours on the radio each Sunday morning we just natter - about topics as diverse as sport, what colour sauce should go on your bacon sarnie and the latest events in Coronation Street. Oh, and every now and then, we talk about tickling your tatties, pruning your pear tree and cultivating your cucumbers (although I much prefer to not to get into male and female plants and what to do with them... far too embarrassing for a young lad like me.) It's a programme I adore, not least because I have endless respect and affection for Joe – but please don't tell him I said any of that soppy stuff.

My invitation to you is to sit back, grab a coffee, read, enjoy and learn, just as we do each Sunday. The difference is you'll always have this book to refer back to, whereas with me on the radio, it goes in one ear and straight out the other.

Joe Maiden? Bless 'im!

**Tim Crowther**
Co-presenter, *Tim and Joe*,
BBC Radio Leeds

# ABOUT THE AUTHOR

Born in Cumbria, Joe Maiden spent many years working for Leeds City Council, becoming a Head Gardener and ultimately a Senior Area Manager looking after many of the city's parks. He also worked with people from the magazine Which?, writing many reports, and displaying vegetables at key Royal Horticultural Society events at Tatton Park, Chelsea and Hampton Court. Apart from his regular broadcasts on BBC Radio Leeds, he is well known for the many hundreds of talks he does for garden societies all over the country.

Joe is married to Betty, whom he praises for her wonderful sense of Yorkshire 'straightforwardness' and love. They have a daughter Sonya and a son John, who is following on in horticulture but ploughing his own furrow.

# Acknowledgements

My special thanks to my wonderful and always very supportive family, my many friends and to all at Great Northern Books – especially the editor David Joy. Also to David & Tim Barritt; Josephine Blackburn; Tim Crowther at BBC Radio Leeds; Steve Ott of Kitchen Garden magazine; RHS Harlow Carr; York Gate garden; and the Yorkshire Post.

Photographs by Jo Axon, David Burrill, Nigel Hall, Jim Smith, Traydarti and Linda Viney.

Photos on pages 17, 19, 21 and 57 reproduced by kind permission of Kitchen Garden magazine.

Joe Maiden and son John, when they won the 'Best in Show' cup at a recent Harrogate Spring Show.

# INTRODUCTION

I have been meaning to write this book for many years. Ever since I first started to broadcast on gardening topics more than forty years ago, I have been asked to set down my thoughts in more permanent form. So here at last is what I trust is the answer to countless requests.

There must be thousands of gardening books, but I like to think this one is very different. Rather than start off with the glamour of flowers, it begins with the far more down-to-earth subject of vegetables. This is partly because they have always been my speciality, but also reflects the fact that they have seemingly become the fastest growth area in horticulture. In an age when the value and taste of home-grown food is at last being appreciated, it is not surprising that interest in vegetables is soaring in the same way as demand for allotments.

That said, I have been determined they should not take over the book. Hence the coverage of a vast range of other subjects ranging from fruit and herbs to bedding plants and hanging baskets, and from lawns to rockeries. Each chapter aims to encourage a hands-on approach with detailed growing guides. Some of the many questions that have come my way down the years are answered in separate sections. As another unusual touch, I decided not to be too

serious and have included several favourite tales with gardening associations.

Humour is after all a special Yorkshire characteristic, and above all I wanted everything in this book to be set in a Yorkshire context. The plants and suggested ways of gardening are as hardy as those who till the soil!

I suppose I am an old-fashioned guy – and especially when I am with Yorkshire folk. One day at one of my lectures I was talking about planting beans twelve inches apart, giving them a pint of water and expecting two pounds of beans from each plant. I realised I was talking old-fashioned English and not metric. So I asked the audience: "Do you prefer feet and inches, pounds and a pint?" Every hand went up! Hence these pages stick firmly to traditional measurements, as conversion tables are readily available for those wedded to metrication.

I am a lucky lad. I have had a lifetime in horticulture and it has never felt to be a job – just a wonderful hobby that became a way of life. I have enjoyed writing this book and hope you enjoy my thoughts and tales.

**Joe Maiden**

Apart from producing wonderful food, potatoes also have vigorous top growth that can stop weeds from growing.

# PART 1. VEGETABLES

# Potatoes

I do not think the main meal of the day is a proper meal unless it has got potatoes with it. I just love spuds – boiled mash, chips or roast – and best of all baby new spuds freshly dug from a Yorkshire garden. This has got to be one of my best moments in the garden in late May, twelve weeks after planting. Place the fork in the soil, ease it back and see the potatoes appear.

I then just walk to my outside tap, wash the baby spuds, and with a bit of a rub the skins come off. Within minutes I walk indoors, hand them to Betty, and twenty minutes later there is an eating experience to behold. Loads of baby spuds and a piece of ham, fresh broad beans and plenty of butter!

## CLASSIFICATION

What is a first early, second early, early maincrop, late maincrop, and salad?

## First Early

These are the types that bulk up quickly. The potatoes are initiated very quickly and varieties like Swift can be ready eight or ten weeks after planting. Most early varieties take approximately twelve weeks.

*Best varieties:*

## Swift

Very early modern scraper suitable for growing in containers, under polythene or glass, and open garden production. Ideal for boiling and for salad use. It is one of the quickest of all potatoes to bulk up.

## Winston

An excellent high-cropping early white potato. Takes about twelve weeks from planting to become big enough to eat. This is the best potato to grow for exhibition work and takes most of the red cards on the show bench.

Freshly dug new spuds – one of the best moments in the gardening year.

Winston – an excellent early white potato.

## International Kidney

A classic heritage variety. If grown on Jersey they are known as Jersey Royals. When lifted early they are small and waxy and mild in flavour. When left in the ground to mature they become large and the flavour is flowery with yellow flesh. They taste great hot or cold – and sliced, diced or eaten whole.

## Mimi

A recently developed variety that produces small uniformed, red salad potatoes. They are round in shape with attractive red skins. Excellent flavour and can be used for boiling and salads.

## Maris Bard

A very popular, tried and tested early variety. The flesh is fairly firm and it is one of the top boiling varieties.

## Pentland Javelin

Very popular early scraper with a good flavour. Must be one of the whitest new potatoes when cooked.

## Second Early

These take between twelve and fourteen weeks but will bulk up well. Lots of second earlies will also store quite well, unlike first earlies which are at their best dug before the end of July.

*Best varieties:*

## Kestrel

The top exhibition variety in the coloured classes. It has long oval tubers, white coloured flesh and white skin with blue eyes. It is possibly one of the best varieties to grow if you have a slug problem.

## Maxine

Excellent quality with shallow eyes and beautiful pink-coloured skin.

## Estima

An extremely popular second early which is a heavy cropper. This variety is popular for early winter storage and its uses are very general regarding cooking.

## Marfona

Extremely heavy cropper. Very useful as a jacket potato. Excellent winter storage.

## Nadine

Said to hold the world record for heaviest yield. I love the flavour of this variety and it is brilliant for jacket potatoes. This is a firm favourite with exhibitors because of its uniformity and shallow eyes.

## Early Maincrop

Can be ready for lifting in August but will grow and make a heavier crop for lifting in October.

**Kestrel – noted for its white skin with blue eyes and resistance against slugs.**

**Nadine is outstanding for jacket potatoes.**

*Best variety:*

## Maris Piper

Undoubtedly the top variety for making chips. Has excellent storage capabilities, and is very popular with the home gardener.

## Late Maincrop

This is the very important crop, grown to store and use in winter and spring until the early varieties are ready.

*Best varieties:*

## Cara

Very high yields, white oval tubers with red eyes. This variety was bred from King Edward and has high blight resistance. Can be a problem in small gardens because of its very vigorous foliage often measuring up to six feet in height.

## Sante

A robust-growing variety, which will cope with a wide range of soil conditions. Very resistant against potato scab. Excellent variety for kitchen use.

## Rooster

Oval tubers with a red skin and yellow flesh, flowery texture and a delicious flavour. Suitable for roasting, steaming, mashing and chipping.

## Salad Potatoes

Now very popular. Often served in restaurants with the skins on and called new potatoes. I still say that a new spud is only new when it first comes out of the soil.

*Varieties often classed as Salads:*

## Charlotte

Very high yielding and with a good flavour. Often used as baby potatoes but on heavy land you will be surprised how large they can grow. An excellent variety.

## Juliette

Raised in the 1990s and classed as an early maincrop. Similar in flavour to Charlotte.

## Anya

This variety was introduced in 1995 and is a Desiree cross Pink Fir Apple. Pleasant nutty flavour without the knobbly characteristics of Pink Fir Apple.

## Ratte

A classic for the French chefs. Wonderful flavour earlier than Pink Fir Apple with no knobbly bits .

## Pink Fir Apple

Raised in 1850 the tubers are knobby and impossible to peel so they are often cooked whole. When cooked they remain firm and they are good hot or cold.

## THROUGH THE YEAR

### Soil preparation

Potatoes really enjoy a good root run in the soil. To ensure this it is a great advantage to prepare your land by digging in large quantities of well-rotted straw manure or garden compost. I like to do this in the autumn. The soil settles during the winter and then you can be off to a flying start. Set your garden line and all that is required is to dig a planting hole six inches deep and lay your potatoes in it.

Apply slug killer into the hole if you have a problem at this stage. When planting potatoes I choose a day when the soil is drying. The reason is so you do not over compact the soil. As already mentioned, potatoes like a free root run.

### Planting time

Many people think that early potatoes have got to be planted very early in the year and late potatoes very late. This is completely wrong. Most gardeners regard Good Friday as Potato Planting Day – especially in Yorkshire. This is only a guideline, give or take three weeks either way. It depends on weather conditions.

I plant all my different types at the same time –

earlies, second earlies, early maincrop, late maincrop and salads. The reason is early potatoes take approximately twelve weeks, second early take sixteen weeks, early maincrop until august and late maincrop from September. Always have your potatoes lifted before frost penetrates the soil.

## Earthing up

This is quite an important job when growing potatoes in early season. Drawing the soil over the young foliage protects it from frost. It also stops the potatoes from going green when coming into contact with the light.

## Lifting potatoes

This is best done with a garden fork, being careful not to stab the tubers. The great advantage of growing your own is that you can lift enough for the one meal so you have supreme freshness. You can buy stale potatoes but not ones that are minutes out of the soil.

## Storing potatoes

Whenever you can, dig fresh and eat as soon after lifting as possible. When it comes to late autumn all potatoes need to be lifted from the soil to be stored through winter, spring and early summer. Potatoes store very well when lifted when mature. Choose a drying day for this task. Some varieties are still in good condition in early July from an October lift. As you lift, lay potatoes on the soil surface and allow to dry for two hours. They can then be put into brown paper sacks and stored in a cool, dark, dry and frost-free area. When you are placing potatoes in the sack, select out any which are not perfect. Use these at once. It is also a good ploy once each month to check through your sacks and remove any blemished tubers. One rotten tuber will soon rot the good ones.

# The Potato Brush and Show Potatoes

My wife Betty used to have a little gift shop. One day she was at a trade fair shopping for some new items to sell and found something that was quite quirky. It was a scrubbing brush in the form of a very lifelike potato. The object was called a 'spud brush' and was fantastic for scrubbing and cleaning potatoes ready for cooking. The top half was coloured and had sunken potato eyes. It was actually like a cross-section of a spud with the short, solid bristle adhering to a bottom flat surface. You had to give these brushes a second look to make sure they were not real spuds.

I now want to go right away from the spud brush and tell you how to grow show potatoes, but I will be back with 'Brushy' at the end of the story.

**Rotted beech leaves are ideal to put in the base of a potato trench**

To grow exhibition show potatoes, or very clean skinned potatoes for jackets, there is one main criteria and that is the medium in which they are grown needs to be well rotted. An effective medium to use is old straw with leaf mould and peat, which retains moisture and prevents the skin being irritated. In time it stops infestations of the dreaded potato scab.

I once remember growing two hundred varieties of potatoes at Golden Acre Park. We opened up trenches twelve metres long, a metre wide and put into the base six inches of well-rotted leaves. We planted the seed potatoes and covered them with three inches of leaves and slug pellets to prevent damage. As the potatoes started to emerge through the leaf mould, another three inches of old leaves was put on along with potato fertiliser (at present I use Sheep-it) and the medium was always kept moist. Potatoes for exhibition can also be grown in perforated bags or twenty-inch plastic pots. It is also a good idea to take the flower trusses off the potatoes as this helps them to set.

Some of the best varieties for show culture are Kestrel which has a purple colouring around the eyes with a white skin; Amour which is an oval potato with a pink splash; Winston, an excellent version of the standard white varieties for eating and show work; Nadine, a beautiful white skinned potato with shallow eyes; and finally Harmony, with shallow eyes which is a good matcher to Nadine. These popular varieties have all superseded the old favourites like Vanessa, Catriona, Di Vernon, Manna and The Bishop.

When potatoes are grown in soil-free compost and lifted, they should always have good, clean, undamaged skin. A good ploy is to cut off the tops sixteen days before you lift, as this gives time for the skins to set. In order to get the perfect set of show potatoes, lift a few tops off very carefully two days before the show. It is a good idea to cut your finger nails so as not to mark the skin. When lifting, place the potatoes into a bucket of water immediately, as this stops the skins from drying out. Next select your matching set along with two spares. You are looking for uniformity, with no slug damage and no scab marks. The following list is what you will require for cleaning the show potatoes:

1. A washing up bowl
2. A Vileda pad (a soft sponge with a harder surface on back)
3. 1 bottle of milk
4. Cotton wool buds
5. 1 egg
6. 1 glass
7. A cardboard plate
8. Soft tissues or toilet roll
9. A pen
10. A cardboard box

## Method of Cleaning

Remove the potatoes from the bucket of water and gently sponge off any soil with the Vileda pad. Use the back of the pad for slightly stubborn marks. When all the soil has been removed, place the selection into the washing up bowl and pour over some milk as this cleanses the skins better than water and it is gentler to the delicate skin. Sponge the potato with a milky pad then get the cotton bud, dip it in milk and gently clean out each eye.

Crack an egg and give the yolk to your dog (our Nelly loves egg yolk) and put the white into a small glass. Dip the sponge into the egg white and gently sponge each potato again and place them flat on a cardboard plate. Keep moving them around on the plate until they look perfect to the eye. Wrap each potato up separately in tissue and number them so that you know in which order they looked best. Put them in the cardboard box and when you arrive at the show place them on the plate in that order. Now sit back and wait for your 'Red Card 1st Prize'. Good luck!

On one of my very large vegetable displays, when I won 'Best in Show', I used forty different varieties of potatoes. Down on the front of the display, each plate had twelve potatoes all dressed with parsley and each variety was labelled (e.g. Potato Kestrel, Potato Nadine etc).

Remember the potato brush? Well, I took with me twelve potato brushes on a plate and set them all up dressed in parsley. I labelled them 'Potato Brush' and set them among my display for a bit of fun. The display was judged by some of the best judges in the country and they could not tell a stone potato from a real one!

*Part 1. Vegetables*

## A Favourite Tale

# Hunters Inn
# Potato Bash

About five years ago I thought it would be nice to raise money for charity using my local pub The Hunters Inn at Pool in Wharfedale. In conjunction with my friend Big Nigel we decided to donate the funds to a local hospice called Wheatfields.

The idea was to give each person a bucket and a potato for a small donation. They had to take the potato away and grow it in the bucket. On August Bank Holiday Sunday we held a charity day when everyone returned to the pub with their buckets for the grand weigh-in. Further monies were raised through the auctions of items donated by the customers, which included handmade decorative walking sticks.

This day was a great success and we decided to make it an annual event. Weights produced have varied from a miserable two ounces to a maximum of 8lb 12oz.

There are many local characters living in the area, all with tales to tell about the event over the years. In Otley a character called David is seen every morning coming out of his house with a jug containing a yellow liquid! He proceeds to feed his potatoes and needless to say he won the maximum weight.

Another character is called Johnny. On tipping out his bucket at the weigh-in it was found to contain a bag of the local supermarket's best potatoes, Needless to say he didn't win.

We have two people, father Stan Cail and his son Stuart, who are keen contestants and strong rivals in the yearly event. They must have a magic potion they use because one of them nearly always wins.

Michael Styrin, the local milkman who is better known as the Mayor of Huby, is a special character. A well-known person in the area, he is a good fund-raiser and supporter of charity work. He has been a friend for many years, always keen to give advice and a good practical joker.

A special thanks to Geoff Nunn, the proprietor of The Hunters Inn, and his manager Carrie for donation of the prizes and use of the pub for the event. Over the years we have raised in excess of £1,000 for charity.

# Parsnips and Carrots

These two crops enjoy similar conditions. Parsnips and carrots like a deep well-worked sandy loam, which has been well-manured for a previous crop. It is a great advantage if it is stone free. I am not asking for much am I!

The pH for parsnips and carrots needs to be 7 which is Neutral. The site is best in full sun. It is advantageous if the ground can be dug over in the autumn and left rough for the winter weather to break it down to a fine crumb structure.

In early February, when the ground is starting to dry out, fork over lightly to break down any clods of earth. At the end of February tread the soil on a dry day and apply two ounces to the square yard of super phosphate and one ounce of sulphate of potash to the square yard. This can then be raked into the top surface.

## Parsnips

Early March to early April in Yorkshire is the best time to sow parsnips. I set the garden line for rows eighteen inches apart. The drill is then taken out an inch deep with a draw hoe. The seed is sown thinly into the drill and covered with soil.

My good friend Dr Carl Denton gave me a good tip, as lots of people have trouble with germination. His advice was to seal in the moisture after sowing by using a plank of wood. Leave it down for three weeks. Uncover within a week and germination should have happened.

Keep moist until the plants appear and watch out for slug damage. When parsnips have made their true leaf formation, start to thin to three inches apart as the season goes on. Use the thinnings as baby vegetables. Keep plenty of distance for the parsnips to swell into good-sized roots.

Parsnips have now become a very popular winter vegetable retaining good condition in the ground until April time. So they can be left in position until you need them. It is always remarked by vegetable gardeners that they improve their flavour with frost.

Lifting a big bunch of carrots grown in a florist bucket.

Varieties:

**F1 Hybrid Countess:** Good against Parsnip Canker.

**White Gem:** Very white flesh, very good quality.

**F1 Gladiator:** Good flavour – best variety of parsnip I have ever grown.

## Carrots

The same ground preparation is needed as for parsnips. I make my first outdoor sowings on April 1st in drills in well-prepared deep soil. Seed is sown thinly in the drills half an inch deep.

Carrots include early varieties for sowing in frames and others for buckets or containers. Some can be grown under a fleece, and there are even round carrots for shallow soils and containers. Finally there are maincrop carrots – stump-rooted, intermediate or long.

**Best varieties:**

For very early carrots the variety Amsterdam Forcing can be sown in the autumn in cold frames or in large pots in the greenhouse.

**Sugarnax:** Early maturing with excellent flavour. Can be sown outdoors in early April.

**Chantenay Royal:** Short wedge-shaped carrot that produces high-quality roots.

**Autumn King:** Superb colour, long heavy roots.

**Paris Market Baron:** Very early almost round roots, good for shallow soil.

**F1 Hybrid Flyaway:** Shows a good tolerance against carrot fly.

Jerusalem Artichokes are one of the easiest vegetables to grow. The only downside is their reputation for playing havoc with the digestive system!

# Jerusalem Artichokes

## Vegetables for Nothing

Some twelve years ago I moved to my new plot and I took six Jerusalem Artichokes. The variety was Fuseau, which has longish tapered tubers and is very productive. I planted the tubers two feet apart in two short rows. I prepared the land by digging in three large barrowfuls of well-rotted farmyard manure. The tubers were planted six inches deep in early March. By mid April they were growing very strongly. I top-dressed the area with four inches of well rotted garden compost. Prior to this I applied three handfuls of blood, fish and bone meal that I hoed in. The plants grew extremely quickly with very strong foliage which totally acted as weed suppressant.

Fortunately I grew the artichokes at the back of my plot because by mid August the tops had grown to over six feet. To keep the plants tidy and upright, I supported them by knocking in some posts with some strand wires and tied in the strong shoots. By the end of September they were nine feet tall and in full flower.

Jerusalem artichokes have a reputation with some people of playing havoc with their digestive system and can cause severe flatulence. Well I am one such person and so in our house they are banned from my diet! When growing this vegetable across the end or side of your plot they can make a useful windbreak. (What have I just written?) It is also a very hardy vegetable that can remain in the ground until you harvest. I dig around the plant with a garden fork being careful not to stab the tubers. By the end of the season you are bound to have left a few tubers and these will re-grow – hence my title 'Vegetables For Nothing'.

Twelve years ago I planted six and we have cropped this area ever since without any re-planting. So for me this is one of the easiest vegetable crops to produce yet I am still banned from eating it! The only problems I have had with this crop are slug damage and mice, which can dig down and nibble the tubers.

### Joe's Tip

*If you want to replant each year try this:*

Lift some good-sized tubers in February and pot one tuber to a six-inch pot. Put in a cold frame or cold greenhouse. When the pot is full of root with some good top growth, late March or early April, they can be planted on well-prepared land. Then just watch them grow!

# Beetroot

Over the years I have been asked to trial many different vegetable varieties. I was quite excited to try two hundred varieties of potatoes and then one hundred of onions. However, I was much less excited when asked to look at fifty varieties of beetroot. "What a waste of time – a beetroot is a beetroot," I thought, assuming they would all be very similar. However, after growing this trial I changed my mind and saw beetroot in a different light.

A row of germinating beetroot seed.

## Soil conditions

I grew the beetroot on the land where I had grown potatoes. This had been well manured with rotted straw manure and lots of beech leaf mould. Beetroot like well-drained conditions but also like to be grown in moisture-retentive material. The land for potatoes can be on the acid side but beetroot grow better on a soil pH of 6.5 to neutral 7. An area of land that has been manured for a previous crop is ideal for beetroot. You may need to lime the soil to increase the pH. Lime is best applied in February. This saves compaction on land that has been well worked.

## Sowing

Try to get your soil ready for sowing in early March – a dry day with some wind and hopefully sun is best. There will be some clods of soil that have not broken down. I like to tread the soil over with my big size eights, keeping my feet close together. Move over the soil with a shuffling movement as this gives the right amount of firmness. All you have to do now is to run a rake over to bring the seedbed to a fine crumb structure.

At this time of year hundreds of germinating weed seedlings are emerging, so on a sunny day prior to sowing time re-rake the seed bed or use a hoe to kill off the weeds. If the weeds are allowed to grow they will choke out the young beetroot seedlings. I take out a shallow drill ¼ inch deep and sow the seed into the drill making it two inches wide. If the soil is dry, water the base then sow the seeds an inch apart as most beetroot seed throw clusters of seedlings. It is a

good idea to cover the seed with dry soil as this suppresses in the moisture for long enough to allow germination to happen.

I have tried different sowing times going on as late as August 1st to see if the beetroot would keep growing through our milder winters. At Christmas time the sowing made on September 1st were thinned out as baby beetroot. The August sowing were maturing and large enough to thin out and use during October. I earth some soil round the developing roots to protect in case of deep-seated frost.

A special way of growing beetroot was explained to me by my friend Paul Kitchenman. Over the years as a National Vegetable Society judge I have judged hundreds of wonderful exhibits. At a recent West Yorkshire Branch of NVS Show, Paul exhibited the variety Pablo. Each beet was brilliantly uniform with a long, slim, single root and bright, clean, young stalks because at shows beetroot is normally trimmed back to three inches and then tied with raffia.

When I asked Paul how he had grown these perfect specimens, he explained that it had come out of a bit of a mistake. He set out to grow some carrots in boreholes but they failed to germinate, so he re-sowed but they failed again. He then sowed Pablo beetroot seeds in the prepared boreholes and achieved the perfect specimens. His sowing date was May 10th and the show date was September 20th.

*Part 1. Vegetables*

Mice can cause serious damage to beetroot.

## Pests

I have found beetroot to be easy to grow with very few pests. Mice can be a problem, eating away at the roots and often just leaving the shell of a skin. Also slugs can eat the young seedlings.

## VARIETIES

### Traditional round red

#### Pablo

Wonderful globe shape. Still in excellent condition when cricket ball size. Of course can be used much smaller. Has very few internal rings.

#### Pronto

Excellent for baby beet production. Matures to a small-size baby beet in eight weeks. I tend to sow

thickly and constantly pull to use over a long period.

#### Boltary

Good resistance of going to seed. Very reliable.

#### Moneta

A monogerm variety. Instead of clusters of seedlings from one seed as with most varieties, they produce just one seedling. Ideal to space sow to avoid thinning out.

#### Bikores

Good for extra early sowing under cloches or main crop. Good flavour.

#### Crimson King

If you like to clear your garden from crops during the winter months, it is an excellent beetroot for storing traditionally in peat and sand.

#### Detroit Globe

Has stood the test of time! Introduced almost a hundred years ago. Good flavour and stores well.

Pronto – excellent for baby beet production.

## Coloured types

### Golden Beet
Excellent variety. Very sweet. Does not bleed when cooked.

### White Ice
It is good to try new varieties. This one was new to me last year when we used it as a warm vegetable with butter. I will certainly grow it again – it is absolutely delicious!

The old Italian variety – Barbabietola Di Chologgia.

### Barbabietola Di Choioggia
Old Italian variety. When cut it has distinctive white rings. It has a mild flavour and is easy to cook.

## Long beetroot

### Cheltenham Green Top
Best grown in deep soil as the roots can be up to two feet long. When selected for exhibition the long-rooted variety are grown in boreholes.

## Half-long and cylindrical

### Forona and Cylindra
Half-long, stump rooted. Easier to slice than normal varieties and very good flavour.

## Beetroot for salad leaves

### Bulls Blood
Now widely used for the production of baby salad leaf. The leaves taste sweet and the dark red leaves are very attractive. As a manager of the Parks Department, I used Bulls Blood beetroot as an edging plant around beds of geraniums with silver-leafed Cineraria Maritima. What a stunning combination!

## Beetroot – an eating experience!
Warm, baby beetroot eaten whole with some new potatoes, plenty of butter, Iceberg lettuce leaves and a piece of fresh salmon.

*Try this for a change:*
**Beetroot in Blackcurrant Jelly**
Betty makes this every Christmas. One blackcurrant Jelly, ½ pint of hot water, ½ pint of vinegar. Cook the beetroot then cut jelly and beetroot into small cubes. Place in a dish, pour over hot water and vinegar. Mix jelly and beetroot together and place in the fridge to set. Wonderful with cold turkey and ham. Not just for Christmas!

*Part 1. Vegetables*

# Peas

As a small boy the highlight of a summer's day was to walk down with my father to his allotment, where he would pick me a handful of peas to shell fresh and eat. The memory of his early summer variety still lingers. He grew Onward, which followed on from Early Onward with a fourteen-day gap between the varieties.

The sheer delight of a handful of freshly-picked peas.

## Soil preparation

Peas grow well on a good medium loam with some lime content. They do well on most fertile soils so long as they have a good deep root run. As they make an extensive root formation, this tells us that soil needs to be deeply dug and plenty of plant food given.

The best time to prepare for the crop of peas is October. Try to dig down to about eighteen inches but do not bring up any sub-soil into the lower reaches. Dig in rotted garden compost and old farmyard manure, then some soil, then more compost and manure, and finally some more soil. This preparation should give good drainage, and will also act as a reservoir for moisture during the time when the plants are flourishing. Peas love moisture, but do not like the roots growing in waterlogged conditions.

Show Perfection - an amazing variety that can produce twelve peas to a pod.

After the October preparation leave the soil for the winter snow, rain and frost to break the lumps down to form a good crumb structure for spring sowing. In recent times we have not had much severe weather, but in the winter of 2009/10 we had over four weeks of snow, frost and very cold nights. My father said we always needed a hard winter to grow good peas and beans. As it killed off all the pests and diseases I think he might have been right. The crops in 2010 were very good.

As peas like lime, in early February I give a dusting to the area and let the rain wash this into the soil. If lime was applied when the first preparations were done and it got in contact with the manure, a reaction can sometimes take place and all the nitrogen will be lost into the atmosphere.

## Sowing

On the ground that was prepared in October and left to settle, on a drying day take out a trench one-foot wide and about six inches deep. Set the garden line and with a draw hoe pull the soil towards you to create the trench. Level the trench bottom with a small garden rake. Sow the peas two inches apart with four rows across the trench. When sown, cover with two inches of soil. Do not fill in all of the trench. Leave the trench depression as this will act as a watering and feeding area. During the growing season, hoe the area between the rows to keep down the weed. Gradually soil will filter back into the trench giving good anchorage to the roots.

The only feed my peas get through the season is sheep manure pellets – one handful to a yard run of row. I start in the trench when I sow, then once every three weeks until flowering time. When you water it breaks down the pellets providing plant food to the roots. The wool fibres in the pellets keep away the slugs.

## Protecting the seed

Birds can be a problem eating the seed so I cover the area with fine-mesh wire-netting. The main culprits are pigeons, jackdaws and crows.

## Watering

There is often enough moisture in the well-prepared soil until flowering time. Over watering up to this time tends to give taller thinner plants. Short stocky plants give more flowers and it is at flowering and podding time when the plants require frequent watering to make every pod swell to full capacity. At this stage the sheep pellets, which are slow release, work well feeding the plants.

When the pods are ready for picking, hold the plant with one hand and disconnect the pod with your other hand. Do this gently so as not to weaken the root system.

## Supporting the plants

I do believe that even the shortest growers require support to keep the pea pods from being soiled. Branches of twigs cut in wintertime and tied in bundles ready for use when you require them are a good idea. When cutting branches select the size you require for specific varieties. Also cut some straight pieces to strengthen the branches in a row. String and wire can also be used for strengthening.

### Joe's Tip

When cutting branches to support peas, form a long point on the base for easy insertion. At this season of the year time is at a premium. In winter you will probably have more time.

I am lucky to have birch trees growing on my boundary. They benefit greatly by thinning the branches each year and these are fantastic. A framework of birch with all the twiggy bits is ideal for supporting peas.

I have also got hazel trees growing, which again make very good supports. You need permission from the landowner to cut trees but if you talk to a tree surgeon I am sure you will find plenty of waste branches.

Another method is to use three-inch mesh wire-netting nailed to posts down to the row. This is an ideal way of supporting because most varieties of peas have tendrils that cling to posts and wire.

## When to support

As with sowing, protect with wire mesh to stop bird damage. As the peas germinate and grow to two inches, take off the mesh. This is the time to support, so place branches in position or twigs and wire mesh. For extra protection from the birds, place black cotton at the base and just wind this into your supports. When a bird touches the cotton, which it cannot see, it is disturbed so it flies away and does not eat your crop. Use a soft cotton that breaks easily and does not tangle around the birds.

## Very Early Peas

I like to sow Felton First Early in September or October. I use plastic segment trays, placing six seeds to each segment, which are planted out on the sheltered plot. I plant each segment, leave about four inches, and then another segment. By putting six seeds to each segment, it allows for any losses during the winter and you can expect fresh garden peas in early May.

You can also sow in large pots in the polytunnel for an extra early crop. Felton First Early can also be sown out of doors in early spring. If necessary cover half the row with cloches and leave half the row uncovered for a crop succession.

### A treat for the gardener of the house

When hanging baskets have passed their best in early autumn, bring them into the greenhouse. Strip out the plants, refreshen the compost and sow sixteen seeds to a sixteen-inch hanging basket. Hang in the cold greenhouse six or eight feet off the ground – it really does confuse the mice. Let them grow and hang down. What a treat for the gardener at the end of April when Felton First Early pods arrive in the kitchen.

*Other good early varieties are:*

### Meteor

Very dwarf so excellent for more exposed areas. Well-filled pods with six to eight peas per pod.

### Pilot

Taller growing variety, very early to mature from an autumn sowing. Can also be sown in the spring.

### Little Marvel

Very sweet flavour.

### Kelvendon Wonder

Heavy crop of small peas. Good for succession cropping.

### Early Onward

Blunt ended pods. Firm favourite over many years – often nine peas per pod.

## Second Early Peas

### Greensage

A semi-leafless variety with good clinging ability. Ten peas per pod.

### Green Shaft

I think now the most popular variety producing pods in pairs, sometimes with ten or eleven peas to a pod.

## Maincrop to Late Varieties

### Lincoln

Curved long-pointed pods, ten to eleven peas per pod, height about three feet.

### Ambassador

Dark green blunt pods. Excellent resistance to powdery mildew and pea wilt. Height 3ft 6ins. Can crop very late in the season.

### Onward

A wonderful variety.

### Show Perfection

How many peas do you like on your plate? You may say forty-eight, which with this variety is just four pods at twelve in a pod. Show Perfection, which is the variety that the showmen use, can grow up to eight feet tall.

We tie them up eight-feet canes and grow them on a single stem. They can crop over a very long period producing very beautiful and sweet peas. I sow in module trays – one per cell. When two inches high I plant one to each cane, nine inches apart in the row.

Showmen grow these on a single stem taking out the side shoots and removing the tendrils so that all the energy goes into the pods. For the table I have grown some fantastic crops of Show Perfection on large wigwams or silver birch twigs – and sometimes show winners.

### Mange tout
Very popular in restaurants. It is an edible podded pea.

### Carrouby de Mausanne
Attractive purple flower. Long large pods up to four inches long, good sweet flavour. Height five feet.

### Dwarf Sugar
Pick and cook whole when about two inches long to achieve wonderful sweetness. Plant height two feet.

## Sugar Snap Type

The great advantage of this type is that you can pick over a long season.

### Delikett
Allow to develop into fully rounded pods, then you can shell and also eat the seed.

### Sugar Snap
Excellent variety. Tall plants four to six feet, three-inch pods, very sweet flavour.

### Waverex Petitpois
Very heavy cropper, masses of pods, very tiny seed, extremely sweet.

# Broad Beans

You either love them or hate them. My family and I love them with potatoes and they have to be my favourite vegetable. New potatoes, broad beans and a piece of ham – my mouth is watering! Broad beans are wonderful in salads, and I also love them cold after they have been cooked.

## Sowing
Broad Beans can be sown over a long period of time beginning in October and November. In spring you can sow from February through until May to give you a succession of picking.

## Ground preparation – autumn sowing
I choose an area of the garden that has grown a previous crop such as potatoes or onions. All I have to do is to fork the area over deeply to break down the lumps. A fortnight before sowing the seeds I apply three ounces to the square yard of bonemeal. Tread the area and sow the seeds nine inches apart. Always sow a few extra beans at the end of the row in case any fail. If a double row is required make two drills a foot apart.

When the seed germinates fill in any gaps with your spare plants. At this stage I place some stout canes at every three yards down either side of the row. As the plants grow, supporting strings are tied to the canes to keep them upright and straight.

The best variety for autumn sowing is Aqudulce Claudia, which will crop from May to June. It is very useful, as a second crop can be produced from the side shoots. These will ultimately flower and produce beans.

You can also sow broad beans in modules using a multi-purpose or John Innes compost. The modules I use are plastic pack sixes. I place two seeds to each segment, which can be germinated in the cold frame or cold greenhouse. I have great success by planting the two germinating beans from each segment together, and then leaving twelve inches before I plant the next two in the same way.

Fresh broad beans make the perfect accompaniment to a meal of baby spuds and a piece of ham.

The great advantage of growing in modules is that you can choose the ideal day when to plant out. Try to plant the beans before they get too tall – about three inches is the ideal size.

## Ground preparation – spring sowing and planting

My method for spring sowing is to prepare the ground in the autumn time. I dig in one barrowload of well-rotted farmyard manure to the square yard. The land should be well drained and allowed to settle in the winter time. Broad beans like some lime in the soil and an ideal pH would be between 6.5 and 7. Prior to sowing and planting, tread and rake the ground to a fine tilth.

## Varieties:

### The Sutton
Excellent if gardening on an exposed site. It is a short growing plant. Also suitable for sowing in the autumn, it will produce six to eight beans to the pod.

### Giant Exhibition
A top variety for the show bench, sometimes with nine to ten beans to the pod. The trick with this variety is to remove the misshapen beans and leave the well-matched specimens to mature into show beans.

### Stereo
Small podded type containing five beans. Very good quality with exceptional flavour, this variety can also be used for cooking whole – like we do with the mangetout pea.

### Aquadulce Claudia
Best variety for over-wintering.

### Masterpiece Green
Very good quality, fine flavour, seven to eight beans per pod.

### Bunyards Exhibition
Possibly one of the heaviest cropping of them all.

### Scorpio
A good late type, eight beans per pod, very heavy cropper, good flavour.

## Saving your own seed
Many allotment growers often save their own seeds of broad beans but only from crops that have done well. Leave the pods on the plants until they go black, and then thoroughly dry before shelling. Keep in a cool dry place but out of the frost until ready for use.

## Broad beans as a green manure
Broad beans are a very bulky source of green manure. Being a legume like peas and lupins, they can be grown on your land and then dug in. The roots have nodules that fix nitrogen so this is a wonderful way of putting something back into the soil. The nodules are caused by bacteria that has the power to fix nitrogen from the atmosphere and create a solid substance. Plants such as lettuces and all the cabbage family, which make large green leaves, therefore benefit greatly from following beans and peas.

# Runner Beans

Before we can look forward to our bumper crop of beans for the plate and freezer, there is some hard work to do in preparing the ground.

## Ground preparation
This starts in October and involves digging out a trench eighteen inches deep and 2ft 6ins wide. I then dig over the bottom of the trench with a garden fork to alleviate any compaction and make sure the drainage is good. Runner beans love moisture, but do not like their roots to be stood in water. Stagnant water in the base of the trench would eventually rot the roots and the plants would die.

October is the month I call 'the changing seasons'. At this time of year we have autumn leaf fall and also the summer bedding plants are failing. Plants like the Busy Lizzy, petunias and so on are removed from the flower beds and with the leaves can be placed at the bottom of the trench.

To this I add one barrowful of fresh 'strawy' farmyard manure or good garden compost to a two-yard run of the trench. This is then mixed in with the green material, the fresh manure activating the rotting process. About a month later I start to backfill with soil that was removed from the trench. I put a six-inch layer of soil over the top, which I then mix into the manure. This is then allowed to settle.

In January I backfill completely using one barrowful of well rotted farmyard manure to a yard run of trench, mixing soil and manure as I do so. The top six inches of the trench is filled with good topsoil. At this stage I like to give a dressing of lime, two ounces to the yard of trench.

## Sowing
It normally takes three weeks from sowing to planting out. In recent years I planted out my first sowing on 28 May for my early crop. My second sowing was planted out on 1 June and my third sowing on 1 July. The latter were planted in my polythene tunnel to give fresh beans late in the year. My last picking was on 20 November.

*Part 1. Vegetables*

Runner beans ready for planting out.

I always sow my runner beans individually in module trays or three-inch pots – I actually prefer pots. The compost can be a good multi-purpose or John Innes No 1. Plant one seed per pot an inch deep. I plant the seed on its side at 45 degrees so the water runs off. If you lay it flat and the compost gets too wet, the seed can become too soggy and rot. A night temperature of not less than 50F is ideal and germination takes about eight days. Once the seed has germinated, grow on in well-ventilated conditions but watch the night temperature.

## Planting out

Prior to planting out, sprinkle two ounces to the yard run of trench of blood, fish and bone meal and one handful of sheep manure pellets such as Sheep-it or Slug Gone. Sheep-it is a slow-release organic fertiliser that works season long. Rake the fertiliser into the soil.

It is at this stage I place my canes in position, eighteen inches apart each way. By now my young plants are growing well with their main shoot already winding around the cane in the pot that acts as a

### Betty Maiden's Tip

Think of winter! When you have plenty of young and fresh beans, get them in the freezer for use in winter time.

trainer. Some gardeners prefer using eight-foot lengths of straight tree branches.

Just before planting, soak the plant in the pot with water. To plant, simply dig out a planting hole slightly larger than the pot size. Knock the plant out of the pot, firm in well covering the roots and, as soon as planted, water the soil well if it is dry. At this stage the plants grow away very quickly. It may be necessary to attach the leading shoot to the cane with string and it will eventually adhere itself.

## Aftercare

Gardeners are frequently disappointed with their beans early in the season when the flowers often fail – a problem known as 'dry set'. The plants will be growing quickly, providing lots of leaves, flowers and side shoots. I recommend you remove the side shoots, as this often alleviates the problem and the flowers will then start to form beans. Sometimes over-watering early on can cause this problem and cold nights are also blamed.

Water regularly. I top-dress with Sheep-it, one handful to the yard run of row prior to watering. As noted in the chapter on Peas, this has a double action – it feeds and also keeps slugs and snails at bay. Sheep-it contains lots of wool fibres that stick to the underside of slugs. This dries them out – and slugs cannot function without moisture.

## Harvesting

Runner beans are very productive, but are best eaten young to avoid stringiness. Regular picking also helps to keep them cropping. Never pull the beans from the plants as you risk breaking the thin stems. Either pinch the stalk with your thumbnail to sever it from the stem or cut the stalk with sharp scissors or a knife.

Pop the pods into a polythene bag and keep them in the fridge until needed or top and tail. Blanch for three minutes before plunging in cold water. Dry with a kitchen towel and freeze in conveniently sized portions.

## Favourite varieties
I have grown most runner bean varieties. The following are some of my favourites:

### Crusader
An old variety that still crops well and has good flavour. Pick young to avoid strings.

### Desiree
White-flowered, fleshy pods almost stringless.

### Enorma
Possibly now the most popular variety, with slender pods of good length. One of the best varieties for the show bench.

Other varieties that have done well for me are Butler, Prizetaker, Lady Di, Liberty, Streamline, Red Rum and White Emergo. Try the variety Hestia in large pots or hanging baskets. This is an attractive bush-type variety bearing red and white flowers and tender pods.

## Pests and diseases
Apart from the problems with flower drop that I have already tackled, Runner beans do not suffer greatly from pests and diseases, but there are a few things to watch.

Growing in trays initially gets over the problem of mice or squirrels eating the seeds. It also reduces damage from pea and bean weevils, which often nibble the leaves, leaving round notches in the leaf edges.

Birds, mainly sparrows, may occasionally nip off the buds, so reducing the crop. White-flowered varieties such as White Emergo and White Lady are a little less attractive to them and should be sown where this is a problem.

Tall and straight tree branches being used to support Runner beans.

*Part 1. Vegetables*

I save from my Enorma plants each year, choosing pods with eight or nine beans in them.

Bean rust causes red and then black pustules to form on the leaves and this can cause reduced vigour. There are no very effective sprays and the best method of defence is to keep the rows well watered and the roots mulched in hot weather.

Red spider mites also tend to strike in hot conditions and watering over the leaves on hot days (in the evening or when the rows are in shade) will deter them. Alternatively, spray with a suitable insecticide, avoiding the flower clusters as much as possible.

Aphids, particularly blackfly, will infest the shoot tips in summer and should be wiped off with finger and thumb or controlled with sprays.

Finally, a bacterial disease called halo blight may appear. This causes black spots to form on the lower leaves and stems and may move up the plants as they grow, eventually affecting the pods too. The spots become dry and are surrounded by a characteristic yellow halo.

Never save seeds from infected plants. Also, avoid soaking seeds before sowing, as this allows the bacteria to spread from one seed to another.

## Save your own seed

My own selection of runner beans goes back twenty years. I had a wonderful row of Enorma given to me by my uncle Harry. I save from the best plants each year, letting the best beans stay on them until they go dry and brown. I choose pods with eight or nine beans in them. At this stage, the pods are removed and left in a warm, dry place. The seed is shelled from the pods and put into packets for sowing the following year. It is a fantastic eater and has won many prizes on the show bench.

## Beans in a bin

There is always the dwarf variety Hestia for those with limited space, but as an alternative a good crop can be grown in an old dustbin with drainage holes in the base. If you have a lawn and need to straighten the edges, put a one-foot layer of turf bits mixed with old manure in the base. Mix with good soil, spent growing-bag material, a sprinkle of lime and some blood, fish and bonemeal. Fill the bin to the top and on 12 May (or thereabouts) sow eight seeds.

Put a sheet of glass or perspex over the bin to act as a mini cold frame and to help germination. Protect in this way, ventilating and covering when needed until the end of May. Thin out the seedlings to the best four plants. Push in four canes – one to each plant – tied to the top to form a wigwam. Water well and feed every fourteen days with a good liquid feed. You will soon be harvesting beans from the bin from very attractive plants.

# Cauliflowers

**A superb cauliflower head showing close curds.**

Many people find great difficulty in producing good quality cauliflowers and all brassicas.

## Ground preparation

Cauliflowers and brassicas require a good rich soil with a pH over 7. Cauliflowers are best grown on land that has not had any of the brassica family on it for at least four years. Rotation is most important because of build up of the disease called Club Root. If you have got this disease in your land it will devastate the crop.

Ground preparation should begin in the autumn time by digging in a good quantity of well-rotted farmyard manure. The ground can then be left in a rough state to allow the winter weather to break the soil down to a fine crumb structure. Frost, rain, wind and snow can work miracles on a heavy clay soil during the winter months.

## Lime

If your soil is deficient in lime it is best put on during the winter months. A good time to apply lime is just after a heavy frost, as during frosty weather there is very little wind. This means the lime can be applied without it blowing everywhere. By applying lime on a frosty morning you can walk on your soil without doing damage by compaction.

## Choice of varieties

There are hundreds of cauliflower varieties, some of which are good for light soil and others for heavy soil. There are varieties for every season of the year and different techniques are required for the different seasons. As might be expected, the most difficult months for producing cauliflowers are in the middle of winter, while the easiest are from June till November.

## Winter and Spring headed varieties

This is the term for cauliflowers that start to head in April, May and June and are often called broccoli.

These varieties will often be quite successful on poorer soil, as they have a longer time to grow and take almost twelve months from sowing to harvesting.

The way to propagate these varieties is to sow them in a seedbed at the end of April and May. The later varieties can be left until June. The seedbed must not have grown any member of the brassica family for at least six years. In fact, I think it best that it should never have had any brassicas on it at all, in order to avoid the dreaded Club Root disease. Sow in drills half an inch wide and twelve inches apart. Sow thinly so that the plants do not get drawn in their early stages. When they are four to six inches high, they are ready for planting in their permanent quarters.

Winter and spring headed varieties include Allsmeer, Snowcap March, Walcheren Winter, English Winter, St George, and Markanta.

## Summer varieties

These are for early cropping and may be sown in a slightly heated greenhouse in January. Alternatively, they can be sown in October and over-wintered in a cold frame to plant out in late March or April. When sowing in a greenhouse in January the temperature should not be lower than 40 Fahrenheit.

Planting out young cauliflowers.

The seedlings can be potted when they are large enough to handle into three-inch pots, or into the plastic coffee cups that you can get from dispensable coffee machines. Remember to put a hole in the bottom of them. Use a compost with no soil. Alternatively sow in October and over-winter in a cold frame prior to planting out in late March.

These varieties crop in June, July and August. They include Clapton (resistant to Club Root disease), Snowcrown (a F1 hybrid), Montano Dok Elgon, and Dominant.

## Late summer and autumn varieties

These are the most popular types, which most people attempt to grow. The best way to propagate is to sow them in a four-inch pot. This is ideal to sow thirty-six seeds into a compost with no soil, then place in a cool greenhouse or garden frame. Good seedlings should be ready ten days from sowing to pot into three-inch pots, again using a compost with no soil, and can be grown in a cold frame until they are ready for planting out.

The cropping period for these varieties is August through to late October. They include: Nevada, Cervina, Dok Elgon, White Satin and White Rock.

## Planting out

The planting out process is the same for all the different types of cauliflowers and all brassicas. Plant summer cauliflowers 18in by 18in, autumn 24in by 24in, and winter 30in by 30in.

Set the garden line and mark out the rows at the correct space by putting in a small garden cane. With a spade, take out a small depression twelve inches square and four inches deep, and work it well with a trowel. With pot-grown plants, take them out of the pot and put them into the depression. Make sure before planting that they have been well watered.

If the weather conditions are dry after planting, thoroughly soak the depression. Protect against slugs and cabbage root fly by using the appropriate deterrent.

This particular method of planting is one I have perfected over many years for all members of the brassica family. The advantages are:

*a) The plant is easy to water and feed in the depression.*
*b) It is easy to protect from pests and diseases.*
*c) As we hoe the area for weed control during the growing season, the depression fills with soil and thus supports the plant well.*

Never allow the plants to dry out as cauliflowers need plenty of water, especially when they are starting to head. Three weeks after planting apply an ounce of nitrochalk to each depression and water in. Six weeks after planting a further application of nitrochalk can be applied. Continue to hoe through the plants to keep the weeds down.

**One of the best of cauliflowers – the top show variety Aviso.**

Cauliflowers form a key part of a superb display of vegetables at Harrogate Spring Flower Show.

33                                                                 *Part 1. Vegetables*

# Cabbages

Cabbages are a member of the brassicas family and selected varieties will give continuity of cropping throughout the whole year.

## Early Summer Cabbages

### Propagation

It is as well to sow Early Summer Cabbages in the gentle heat of a greenhouse with a night temperature of not less than 40F. It is best to sow the seed in a compost with no soil because of the dreaded Club Root disease. This could be in the garden soil, and if a young plant was infected in the early stages it would not grow successfully. For normal garden situations it is not necessary to sow a large amount of seeds of one variety. You can soon fill your garden with cabbage plants that would all mature at the same time. It is far better to use varieties that will give you a continuity of cropping.

My method is to use a four-inch pot filled solely with sterilised compost, which is watered well the night before you sow the seed. Such a pot is large enough to germinate thirty to thirty-six cabbage seedlings. After sowing the seeds sift a fine layer of compost over them to a depth of about an eighth of an inch. Then cover the pot with a sheet of newspaper to avoid excessive drying out.

After about four to six days the seedlings should have germinated. Immediately after germination has taken place remove the newspaper and stand the pot on a shelf in the greenhouse, near to the glass to avoid the seedlings becoming drawn. For strong and healthy plants I think it is necessary to put the seedlings into individual plant pots or cell pots. A good and cheap method is to obtain disposable plastic cups from coffee vending machines (as noted under 'Cauliflowers').

Again, use only sterilised compost and pot the young seedlings before they have made their true leaves and are about an inch tall. Grow them on in the gentle warmth of the greenhouse for about ten days

and then transfer to a cold frame. Keep the frame ventilated to start the hardening-off process prior to planting out. This is done in the same way as cauliflowers.

Planting distances are twelve inches apart with eighteen inches between the rows.

*Varieties:*

### Hispi (F1 Hybrid)
The earliest Summer Cabbage, which matures in late May from indoor sowing. A compact and pointed-headed variety that is deservedly very popular. Its main fault is that it does not stand too long when mature.

### Greyhound
A very high quality and quite a solid variety with pointed heads.

### Derby Day
Possibly the best dark green ball-headed variety for raising under glass for early planting out. Sow March or April for early summer cutting. More resistant to bolting than other Summer varieties.

### Quickstep (F1 Hybrid)
Very reliable and remains in top condition without splitting for eight weeks or more, long after other Early Cabbages have gone over.

### Golden Acre
An improved strain of Primo. An excellent ball-head variety, very heavy and solid. Slightly earlier than Quickstep but does not stand as well.

## Late Summer and Autumn Cabbages
These varieties can be sown out of doors in a prepared seed bed in March, April and May. Choose a site that you know to be clean and free from disease.

Rake down to a fine tilth and sow the seed in drills twelve inches apart. If the weather conditions are dry at this time of the year, make sure the seedbed is kept moist. Most home gardeners favour sowing in the pots or transplanting into individual pots, as with Early Summer Cabbages.

The method of growing on and planting out is also the same. Planting distances are eighteen inches apart with two feet between the rows.

### Minicole (F1 Hybrid)
Light green outer leaves, globe-shaped with a little core. Remains in good condition for months without splitting.

### Kilaton (F1 Hybrid)
New variety with Club Root resistance.

### Winnigstadt
Matures October, extra pointed heart, exceptional taste.

## Winter Cabbages
The sowing, planting and growing on is exactly the same as for the Late Summer and Autumn Cabbages. Sow between April and May. Varieties are listed below in order of maturity.

### Christmas Drumhead
Dwarf compact, ready October to November.

### January King
Red-tinged heads, ready November onwards.

### Celtic (F1 Hybrid)
The large solid heads remain in good condition without rotting or splitting for a very long time.

### Polinus (F1 Hybrid)
Ideal for winter use. Wonderful cabbage for coleslaw and salads.

### Holland Winter White
Extra late and very hardy.

Kilaton – a new variety of cabbage resistant to the dreaded Club Root disease.

## Red Cabbages
Cultivation as for Late Summer and Autumn Cabbages.

### Ruby Ball (F1 Hybrid)
Outstanding for quality and flavour. Uniform and solid. When sown in April is ready in August and will stand until the New Year.

### Red Dutch
Very hardy and ideal for pickling.

### Aurora
Very large heads and a small internal core.

## Savoy Cabbages
Sow as for Winter Cabbages, with the same type of cultivation.

### Savoy King (F1 Hybrid)
An early Savoy, ready for cutting from late September onwards. Heads are very large with distinct light green colour.

*Part 1. Vegetables*

Aurora – a Red Cabbage with a very large head.

Durham Early is a Spring Cabbage noted for its small and firm head.

### Winter King

Quality stock with finely crinkled dark green leaves. Extra solid hearts. Mid-season maturity.

### Ormskirk and Ormskirk Late

Hearts in January/March. Very hardy and solid and a lovely flavour.

### Wivoy (F1 Hybrid)

The best late Savoy. The hearts are round, dark green and firm with nicely crinkled leaves. All the plants produce firm hearts, without any rosette types, and can stand until the end of April. Withstands frost better than any other kind.

## Spring Cabbages

Often known as Spring Greens, this is the ideal crop to follow Early potatoes. Rake the ground after the potatoes have been lifted. If necessary apply a dressing of lime three weeks before sowing to raise the pH of the land to above 7. If lime has been applied and ground conditions are dry, water the land well and then rake it down to form a fine seedbed. It may be necessary to firm the ground by treading with your feet prior to raking.

Seed can be sown in drills fourteen inches apart from the last week in July until late August. Seedlings can be thinned out to the required spaces. Alternatively sow in a seed bed and transplant when the plants are about four inches high. The spacing depends on whether you want to produce masses of Spring Greens or hearted Spring Cabbage.

My method is to sow the cabbages quite thinly. As they mature, pull out and use as required, leaving in strong plants to grow on and make hearts. If you do transplant Spring Cabbages make sure they are well watered until they become established.

*Varieties:*

### Durham Early

Small firm heads, quite beefy.

### Flower of Spring

Quick to mature, good autumn greens.

### Spring Hero

First ball-headed Spring Cabbage. Often produces heads over 2lb in weight.

# Brussels Sprouts

### Ground preparation

All cultivations are the same as for cauliflowers and cabbages. The sowing date for Brussels Sprouts is from the end of March until end of April. The only different criteria is that when planting out I make sure they are given plenty of room to grow and therefore are 2ft 6in apart. When planting Brussels Sprouts I use the same method as for all other brassicas by planting into a depression. I make sure that they are planted firmly and water well until they get established.

I now wish to make a statement, namely that Christmas dinner would not be the same without sprouts. Turkey without them is like rhubarb without custard.

A successful crop of Cavalier Brussels Sprouts

Oliver is a very early Brussels Sprout.

*Best varieties:*

**Oliver**
Very early Brussels Sprout maturing from August onwards.

**Maximus**
Good variety producing from September until Christmas time.

**Cavalier**
Excellent Sprout for October, November and December.

**Wellington**
Excellent, with late cropping from January until April.

**Bridget**
First class with good-shaped buttons.

**Rubine**
If you like something a bit different, this is a red sprout with excellent flavour.

All the varieties of sprouts I have mentioned are F1 Hybrids and far superior to some of those of yesteryear. They all form firm buttons from top to bottom and stand over a very long period without blowing.

*Part 1. Vegetables*

# Calabrese

*This is the green broccoli. Varieties include:*

**F1 Arcadia**
Ready for early cutting between 70 and 85 days.

**F1 Chevalier**
One of the top varieties for summer use.

**F1 Emerald City**
Very versatile and very quick maturing. Ready in 70 days from planting.

**F1 Marathon**
A late variety sown from late June to early August to be ready early October to November.

# Purple Sprouting Broccoli

Normally sown April and May to be ready the following spring. Very useful as it crops when vegetables are scarce.

Purple Sprouting Early is a very useful variety for March cutting. Purple Sprouting Late can be cut from the end of April.

Two new varieties are Red Arrow and Rudolph. Superior to the older varieties, they are both F1 Hybrids. Something a bit different is White Sprouting broccoli, which is ready in early March.

The distinctive leaves of Dwarf Green Curled Kale.

Redbor Kale would not look out of place in a flower garden.

The long and blistered leaves of Black Tuscany – a 'brilliant vegetable'.

# Kales

I cannot finish the section on brassicas without mentioning kales known as borecole:

**Dwarf Green Curled**
A superb green kale and very old. In fact I think I was weaned on it!

**F1 Winterbor**
Very hardy type with dark blue-green and finely curled leaves.

**F1 Redbor**
An extremely attractive vegetable, this red-leafed variety could be at home in a flower garden.

I am going to finish the brassica section with Black Tuscany, or the Palm Tree cabbage known as Nero de Toscana. Wonderful in flavour, it has long and heavily blistered green leaves. Fantastic when grown as an ornamental plant in pots in the garden, it is a brilliant vegetable.

# Onions

**The fantastic interest at shows in very large onions is truly amazing.**

I am connected with organising and judging shows exhibiting large displays of vegetables. It never ceases to amaze me about the mystique that onions create – especially the very large exhibition types. I have the great honour of being the MC at the Harrogate Autumn Show each September presented by the North of England Horticultural Society. The National Vegetable Society's Northern Branch provides the judges and stewards and looks after the vegetable section under the watchful eye of their vice-chairman Malcolm Evans.

I oversee the judging of the heaviest onion competition. The amount of interest shown in this vegetable begins with the weigh-in. You just cannot get near the scales and the world record now stands at sixteen and a half pounds in weight.

Onions are not a difficult crop to grow but correct ground preparation is very important. I like to start my preparations in October by digging over the plot and incorporating one large barrowful of well-rotted straw manure to a square yard. Dig this through the soil avoiding deep thick layers of manure and remove any stones.

Stones can cause damage to swelling bulbs. The grazing from a stone can split through the onion skin and Botrysis rot can set in – even months later in storage. When digging in manure in October it is not necessary to break down every clod of soil, as the winter weather frost rain snow will do this job for you.

In February choose a drying day and then tread the soil over with your feet in a shuffling movement. This breaks down any lumps helping them to form a nice crumb structure. Over the next few weeks keep raking the ground, which will then give you an ideal planting surface. Also by raking frequently this movement will disturb any germinating weed seedlings and save lots of hand weeding during the growing season.

My onions grow well on my pH levels (the scale of lime in the soil). My pH is 6.8. If you need to apply lime, February is a good time.

*Part 1. Vegetables*

# DIFFERENT TYPES OF ONIONS

## Large or exhibition types

Many exhibitors now save their own seed from good specimens. Over a good number of years, Robinsons Mammoth Ailsa Craig selections and the Kelsae have been the top show types, but the large onions are also fantastic for the table as in most cases they are sweet, juicy and mild.

The top showmen have their own methods. In general terms onion seed is sown through December till January and is often grown in J1 seed compost or a favourite multipurpose compost. Often the seedlings are potted in small pots. I like to pot mine when they are coming into the second leaf. To get maximum size the top showmen grow them on under lights. Some would say twenty-four hours of electric light for three weeks and then twelve hours for a further three weeks. This is giving them wonderful growing conditions during the time of the year when natural light intensity is poor. They are often planted out in specially built growing areas under cover with raised beds created out of breeze blocks and with underground heating and water systems.

Good results can be obtained by sowing in a propagator at Christmas time and growing on steadily, starting with a heated greenhouse and then a cold greenhouse in March/April. They are weaned off in the cold frame and planted out end of April.

## Autumn onion sets

To produce the first mature onion crop of the season you can plant onion sets in the autumn. These are hardy over-wintering onions, which are mature in early summer. For the last twelve years I have been very successful and I have lifted my crop late June or early July. The majority of the crop weighs between eight ounces and a pound.

I have always grown the crop where I have lifted my Second Early potatoes. My potato crop was grown on land with plenty of moisture retentive material and it needs to be well drained. Add lime ten days before you plant the sets if the pH is less than 6.5. Tread and rake the soil for a level surface. I like to plant autumn onion sets close together. Thry can be thinned and used as baby onions or as salad onions by removing the shell.

My advice when planting onion sets is to make a hole with the tip just showing above the soil level. Then tread gently down the row to firm in the sets. If you just push them into the soil you sometimes form a solid area below. The sets cannot root where it is very hard so they pop out of the ground as they try to root.

*Varieties:*

### Radar

Has been around for many years and still one of the best excellent keepers. I have lifted in June/July and still had good sound onions in April and May, so if you grow enough Radar you can be self-sufficient.

### Electric

This is a red onion, flattish to globe in shape, with a splash of red rings when sliced.

## Onion sets for spring planting

Either use land that has been well manured for a previous crop or just add two ounces to the square yard of high potash general fertiliser and lime if required. Or prepare land in the autumn making sure it is well drained. Dig in well rotted straw manure – one barrowful to the square yard.

*Planting:*

To get off to a flying start with planting I place the sets in module trays in January in the cold greenhouse using J1 No1 or a good multipurpose compost. When they start to grow I transfer to a cold frame and ventilate. As the prepared area dries out, gradually tread and plant the spring onion sets.

*Varieties:*

### Turbo

A very good globe-shaped onion and also a very good keeper.

### Sturon

Excellent storing capabilities, very crisp flesh, good shaped bulbs.

Planting spring onion sets in module trays can give them a flying start.
These are now ready for planting out.

**Red Baron**

The best red onion I have grown. Mild in flavour. Plant when the soil has warmed up to avoid bolting.

**Stuttgart Giant**

A flat-bottomed onion. One of the first types to be grown from sets. Going out of favour because of its shape.

*Planting out:*

Rake the area over. The ideal day is when it is dry and the soil surface is drying out.

Take out a planting hoe, press the well rooted modules into holes about six inches apart and with one foot between the rows.

*Growing on:*

For weeding down the centre of the rows use the hoe to kill off weed seedlings. Hand weed close to the plants four hours after hoeing. If dry, water the bed to minimise root disturbance. On a dry day, four hours is sufficient for a good kill of weed seedlings.

*Harvesting:*

Most books tell us to bend down the tops of onions to help ripening. I have never done so and instead allow the tops to go down naturally. The onions are then lifted with both the tops and roots in place and laid on benches to ripen off. A bit of the withered top is easy to fasten into an onion rope if this is your preferred method of storage. Onions can also be stored in trays – or in ladies' tights! They need to be kept cool and dry in a frost-free shed or garage.

## Onions from seed

The seed can be sown in a heated greenhouse in January, February and March (temperature 55 - 60 F). Using J1 seed compost or a good quality multipurpose type, prick out into modules and lower the night temperature as the onions develop. Move into a cold frame to finish off the hardening process, prior to planting out on good land that is free-draining but moisture retentive.

*Part 1. Vegetables*

Welsh Onions will do well in containers but even better in fertile soil.

Onion growers often sow the seed direct into well-prepared land with a fine finish, creating a good seed bed that is then covered with film or fleece to establish germination quickly. Another way I have tried successfully is to sow five seeds to a module. When established these are planted close together. This is a great way of producing a heavy crop of smaller onion.

*Some excellent types from seed (those I have grown recently):*

### F1 Golden Bear
A large globe-shaped onion that is tolerant to downy mildew.

### F1 Arthur
New to me in 2009. Good quality, round globe shape.

### F1 Kardal
Hybrid variety. Can be grown from pellet seed making sowing easy.

### Utah Jumbo White
A large globe-shaped onion that matures late season.

### F1 Toughball
Very tolerant to downy mildew and botrytis. Still wins on the show bench in the classes for smaller onions.

### F1 Hystar
In storage the best I have grown. Very vigorous good quality.

## Pickling onions
Paris Silver skin is a small dual-purpose onion. It can be used as a bulbing onion or for pickling.

## Salad onions
Best grown on land well manured for a previous crop. Sow in shallow drills and start to use when young by thinning out. The thinnings can go into salads. They are then in use over a long period.

### White Lisbon
Best sown from March to July in order to have Spring onions throughout the summer and autumn. Winter hardy White Lisbon should be sown in the autumn for early use.

### Crimson Forest
Red stalked bunching salad onion mild in flavour. Summer type.

### Ishikura
Japanese bunching onion. Long white stem with short green tops, very mild flavour, best in summer time.

### Ramrod
For use all the year round, good winter hardiness. Long white stems.

## Perennial or Welsh Onions

A clump forming onion with a swollen bulbous base and a very strong flavour. Propagation is easy – lift, split and plant. Does well in containers but is much better when planted in good fertile soil.

# Onions to London

**M**any years ago in the demonstration garden in Golden Acre Park, I grew one hundred different varieties of onions, shallots and garlic. I grew these to compare differences between varieties to see if one outperformed another, looking closely at shape, size and colour, carefully monitoring pest and disease control. The end results were to be reported in Which? magazine, along with many other new and old varieties of flowers and vegetables, all from the demonstration garden.

The onion crop performed excellently on our well-cultivated land. During the summer months they were frequently admired by hundreds of visitors to the park. I remember the early part of the season was quite cold and wet and the onion varieties were all planted out by May 10th and soon got established in these ideal conditions. In late June the temperature soared and the onions started to bulb up well, but by July 10th a hosepipe ban was ordered so the crop could not be watered. By August 1st the crop had stopped growing but had achieved a good size. I was watching the weather each day as the soil was so dry. I was worried the rain would come making the onions re-grow but I wanted to keep them on the land so that our visitors could see the finished crop.

Fortunately, the weather was still good by August 20th and the onions had totally dried off so they were lifted and displayed in the greenhouse with labels on for the visitors to view. The onions looked spectacular and it was then I had a brainwave. 'Would Which? magazine allow me to take the onions to London to show on their behalf in the Royal Horticultural Society Halls at Westminster? The news was good and I had permission to show off the onions at the October show.

Over the next few weeks I carefully prepared different varieties like Marshalls, Fen Globe, Kelsa and many others. The onions were ripened off to a full untorn skin and carefully tied with raffia, then selected into matching sets of three or five from each variety. Uniformity and condition are important when showing any vegetable and will score well when being judged.

The excitement started to grow as the show neared and I suddenly started to worry. How was I going to get a hundred varieties of onions to London with no broken skins all in good condition? At that time we had a white BMW estate car, Betty's 'pride and joy'. I dropped all the seats down to give me as much room as possible and I started to pack the bulbs into stacking crates using white polystyrene chips to avoid damage.

I eventually got all the smaller varieties in but we had a problem with the last layer. This comprised very large Kelsae and some extra big versions of my own saved types, some of which were my father's selection many years ago. So the top layers of onions, some weighing six pounds, were sitting in the stacking crates of polystyrene chips on top of all the others. To make the onions look a bit special I gave them all red dickey bow ties fastened around their necks. These were not proper bow ties but were part of our previous Christmas decorations. The onions appeared very smart indeed, looking out of the windows of Betty's 'pride and joy', so we set off Sunday lunchtime to stay in London for the duration of the show.

On the way to the show I had a previous booking; to judge the giant onion competition in Worsboroughdale near Barnsley. The winner was a Scotsman so we accepted some hospitality, which resulted in me having some whisky and giving Betty the responsibility of driving. When we got to her 'pride and joy', we opened the car doors and in the warmth of the afternoon the onions were sweltering enough to bring a tear to my eye. Wow... what a smell!

After a few minutes on the motorway the large onions, staring out of the window in their bow ties, began to attract attention. Passing motorists began beeping their horns and with the movement of the tyres on the road the onions nodded back in approval. Further into the journey the smell of the onions, shallots and garlic was getting very strong, so Betty decided to open the sunroof. The blast of air flowing through the car was so strong that the polystyrene chips holding the onions in place started floating out of the roof of the car. It was like a snowstorm going down the M1!

After many wrong turns we eventually got into the RHS Halls at Westminster. We took all the onions out of the car ready for staging Monday morning. By 5pm they were all in place, some with dickey bows and all the rest looking very well with detailed variety labels.

I quickly noticed people were giving the display close attention and so I left the RHS Halls feeling very proud. I made sure I went back, as good show men do, half an hour before judging on Tuesday morning to make sure all was in order. After a good spray down they were left for the judges to do their business and we returned at midday for the results.

Yes! We had done it – and at our first attempt too. We had won Gold medal. The best bit though was six weeks later when the medal arrived and I read the inscription: 'RHS Gold Medal to Joe Maiden on behalf of Which? Magazine'. When we turned the medal over it said: 'For onions.' I like that.

The following year we took two hundred varieties of spuds and won another Gold medal, but that's another story.

# Garlic

Garlic is a vegetable that builds me up physically and drags me down socially when I am near to the ladies. Many people are amazed that we can grow garlic very successfully in this country, as they think of it being delivered from far-off places. Garlic is a native of Southern Europe and the family group is the lily. Over the last forty years it has become more popular, but before then its culinary uses were confined to the continent. In Britain in those days it was regarded as being slightly improper because of its odour and intense flavour.

Now its popularity for flavouring has increased and, with modern day cuisine being more adventurous, fresh bulbs of garlic are one of the items on the weekly shopping list. But there is no need for it to be on this list as it is very easy to grow. With it being very hardy it can be planted in the autumn or the spring. If in the autumn, especially an early September planting, the cloves will root easily and soon get established.

## Ground conditions

Garlic preferably loves to be grown on well-dug, well-manured, well-drained land. If your land is on the heavy side I would suggest planting is done in springtime but sometimes it is a good idea to pot the cloves in September. Grow them in pots of multipurpose compost through the winter and place in the cold frame. This needs to be adequately ventilated to keep the plants growing well. They are best put into five-inch pots where they should root very quickly .

When the weather conditions are good, plant out in March. I have done this most successfully and very large bulbs have been dug in July. I once won the class with two bulbs at Leeds Show in early August, and the same batch was displayed at Harrogate Spring Show. The following April I was able to show a basket of thirty bulbs in good sound condition.

I have saved my own segments from my best bulbs for a few years. As soon as they start to become inferior I will renew the stock. Always buy garlic bulbs from a reputable stockist. I think it is very chancy to plant supermarket garlic as we do not know the source or the variety, or how long it has been harvested, and it may also be infected with a virus.

## Planting

A good bulb of Garlic can provide anything between nine and fifteen good-size cloves. These can be planted directly into the garden in September, or grown through the winter in pots or modules in the cold frame or the cold greenhouse. When planting, split off the cloves with finger and thumb and divide them down to individual segments. You can plant direct into the garden or into the pots and modules already mentioned. Compost can be John Innes No 1 or a good multipurpose type.

When plants are going direct into the garden I put them close together and thin out so as eventually to leave them about nine inches apart. Use the thinning as baby green garlic fresh from the garden. When lifted, cut off the older leaves and peel back to expose the white piece of blanched stem with the embryo bulb at the base. It is deliciously sweet and not as pungent.

Elephant Garlic, which often makes a huge bulb as big as your fist.

*Varieties*

### Thermidrom
You can plant from November to February, often as many as eighteen segments to a bulb. Ready from July to September.

### Solent White
Huge bulbs often between two and three inches across. Excellent storage variety.

### Purple White
Fewer segments than Solent. Large individual cloves known for lack of bitterness.

### Albigensian White
Originated from Southern France, very large bulbs.

### Iberian White
Can be planted in autumn or early spring. One bulb will give you about ten segments.

### Chesnok White
Said to originate from the Ukraine. Can be planted in September or left until January. One of the earliest varieties to mature – often ready in June.

### Elephant Garlic
Not really a garlic but related to the onion family. Makes a huge bulb often as big as your fist. Great for roasting, but not as strong in flavour as other garlics. In recent years I have judged some fantastic specimens on the show bench. People visiting the shows have been amazed at the size and the good shape of the bulbs, each containing only about six segments.

## Joe's Tip
Produce baby garlic in florist buckets or large pots. Fill a container with compost and push in at least fifty segments close together. With the tips just showing, grow on in a greenhouse to establish. Start to thin as soon as they have made six inches of top. This way you can use the developing garlic over a long period, leaving six in the bucket to develop into mature bulbs.

# Leeks

Leeks are an extremely versatile vegetable that can be produced almost all year round. They are one of the most hardy of all our vegetables and can withstand anything the elements throw at them.

Leeks can be very expensive to buy and often difficult to clean as soil gets down between the skins. This is often due to growth on a field scale with mechanical cultivation. Following a few simple guidelines, leeks are easy for the home gardener to produce and clean without soil between the skins.

**For exhibition work, leeks are best grown from small plantlets known as pips.**

## Sowing

I sow leeks from January through to August. Sowings made between January and March should be made in a greenhouse where the night temperature is between 55 and 60F. Sowing medium should be either seed compost or a suitable multipurpose compost. When the seedlings have germinated and are large enough to handle, they can be transplanted into modules or small pots. When the leeks are growing away strongly, place them in a cold frame until they are large enough to plant out.

Sowing of leeks outdoors should be from mid-March to August. They should be sown in drills ¼ inch deep. The outdoor seedbed needs to be good, clean, fine soil with moisture retentive material added. Well-rotted garden compost is ideal.

## Joe's Tip

If the soil is dry when you have taken out the drill, water it and sow the seed, and then back fill with the dry soil. This will lock in the moisture until the seedlings have germinated.

## Planting Out

When the early leeks from pots and modules are ready for planting, ensure you leave the root ball intact and plant with a trowel. But when grown outside from a seedbed these can be lifted with their bare roots. My method is to take out a small trench about six inches deep then go down say four inches with a dibber. Place the leek plant in the dibber hole and water in. This ensures the soil is washed onto the roots to anchor in the bare roots. The lower leaves should be just sat on the surface. Already there is potentially ten inches of blanched stem.

If extra blanch is required, use a collar of plastic pipe or drainpipe. These could be off-cuts you may find lying around.

## Ground Preparation

Leeks make a large root system and like rich land. Prepare the area well in advance by digging in plenty of old farmyard manure. The old-fashioned method of trenching still works for me.

Take out a trench fourteen inches deep. Fork the base of the trench so the roots can penetrate. Mix in the manure with soil so that a dense layer of manure is avoided. Preparation should be done well in advance of planting to give the soil and manure time to settle and become compact. Use one barrowful of manure to a two yard run of trench. Apply one and a half ounces of blood, fish and bone meal three weeks before planting and rake in thoroughly. My leeks always grow well on a pH of 6.8.

## Pests and diseases

The following will all affect leeks:

| | Use |
| --- | --- |
| **Slugs and Snails** | Slug pellets |
| **Aphids** | Systemic insecticide |
| **White Fly** | Yellow sticky glue traps |
| **Red Spider** | ditto. |
| **Thrips** | Systemic insecticide |
| **Rust** | Systemic fungicide |
| **White Rot** | ditto. |

Plastic collars or off-cuts from pipe lagging can be useful when growing leeks.

## Baby Leeks

These can be grown in florist buckets with holes in the base or in open ground. Start to thin out the leeks and you can eat them when they are thicker than a pencil. Baby leeks are an eating experience to behold! Compost needs to be well drained but moisture retentive.

## Joe's Tip

You can also use baby leeks in salads instead of spring onions. They are much milder in taste yet still delicious.

Using a dibber to plant leeks.

*Part 1. Vegetables*

*Varieties I have grown recently:*

**Jolent**
Very early and excellent for mini veg.

**Hannibal**
Fast grower for summer production.

**Lyon Prizetaker**
Matures early autumn.

**Giant Winter**
Stands well with thick stems. Ready from January onwards.

**Carentan**
Ready from October to January.

**Bandit Blue**
Green foliage. Ready January till May.

**Blue Solaise**
Dark blue/purple leaves. Ready March till May.

*A Favourite Tale*

# Leeks that went missing

One day Barry, a policeman friend from the North East, visited my garden and saw some of my pot leeks growing. He was impressed because his dad was trying to win the local show classes and was looking for a good strain. I said I would grow some on for him in containers. During early summer Barry visited my garden again and saw the large leeks. He was going to take them in October so his father could grow them on and get young plants for the following year.

In my garden I had the best show vegetables I had ever grown – onions, leeks, celery, peas, carrots, parsnips and so on, plus the pot leeks in the containers.

Early in the year a young man from a local village started phoning me up for garden advice and was especially interested in show vegetables. I invited him to come and see me, so as to sort out some vegetables to grow himself, and he visited my garden during the summer.

In early August I went to my garden one Saturday morning and to my horror all my best vegetables had been stolen. These included the pot leeks I was growing for the policeman's dad. On the Saturday lunchtime I went to judge a village show near York. On the way back I saw a banner advertising Thorner Show, so I paid a visit because this is where the young man lived. I thought I would see how he had done.

When I entered the hall a friend of mine, George Horne, had been judging. He said to me: "Joe, there is a young man in here, done very well. In fact he has got some vegetables as good as yours."

The young man was on the stage receiving his trophies. Then he saw me – and the colour in his cheeks faded. I glanced at the show benches and saw my onions, celery, carrots and other vegetables. He had been to my garden, stolen my vegetables and shown them in his name.

On the way back I visited his garden and noticed the leeks grown for Barry's dad were pulled out of the containers and laid in the sun wilting. I arrived home and phoned Barry, who said to me: "I am on holiday but will take you on Sunday morning to his house to confront him." The young man owned up to the crime and Barry arrested him. Later he was fined £50.

In the spring I was able to send Barry's dad some young leek plants. Barry moved on so I may never know how these leeks grew. So stealing show produce from gardens does occur because it happened to me. The joys of horticulture!

You have to forget things like this and get on with it. The following year I was Northern Champion at Bakewell Show.

# Tomatoes

I would like to bet that in Great Britain there are not many gardens with a greenhouse that do not have a few tomatoes growing in them during the summer months. The taste and smell of a home-grown tomato picked when it is warm is something very special.

Tomato plants can be very delicate and in the first few weeks of growth as seedlings they need warmth, humidity and the right care and attention. If you have the luxury of a heated greenhouse, very early crops can be achieved. If you have an unheated greenhouse, planting in milder areas can start in March, but watch the weather forecast and give extra protection if the night temperatures dip.

## Sowing

Tomato seed can be very expensive. Some of the F1 hybrid types can cost 25p for one seed. Take care of your seed by sowing correctly. Depending on your conditions for growing on, in either a heated or unheated greenhouse, sowing can start early in the New Year. You need to maintain a temperature of 60F.

My method is to sow twelve seeds to a four-inch pot. They are large enough to handle so you can space the seed. The compost I use is a good quality, multi-purpose type and the prepared pots are watered the night before sowing. After sowing, press the seed into the compost. Then cover over with fine compost. In general terms, the covering is twice the thickness of the size of the seed. Place in a propagator or on a heated bench in your home or in a greenhouse.

I prefer to sow a few seeds in a four-inch pot as stated above. However, you can sow individual seeds in a cell tray if you wish – it is personal preference. Young tomato plants are grown on in warm conditions in individual pots.

Freshly picked home-grown tomatoes have a very special taste and smell.

## Transplanting seedlings

When the seedlings have made two good seed leaves, carefully lift out of the compost. I have an old dinner fork, which is useful for this purpose. When handling seedlings, hold the leaf and not the stem. The plant will always grow another leaf but will never grow another stem. Do not therefore bruise the stem. Pot on individually into small pots. My father always used three-inch clay pots for this purpose – and so do I.

Grow the plants on in good light and maintain warmth. A heated greenhouse or a windowsill indoors will be fine. Wash the greenhouse glass if necessary to allow the optimum amount of light to enter. This is most important early in the year to prevent young plants becoming leggy. If growing on a windowsill in the house, make sure it is in the brightest room. Tomato plants when grown on should be good, firm, squat and short-jointed. They will then give you more trusses of fruit.

Preparing a growing bag for tomatoes.

## Step by step planting: Growing Bag method

1. The first task is to cut the bottom out of two florist's buckets.
2. Then cut two circular holes in the top of the growing bags.
3. Screw the buckets into the growing bag so they feel secure.
4. Top the buckets with more growing bag compost. Plant one good plant to each bucket, leaving a two-inch gap at the top. This will hold sufficient water for the growing bag and percolate right into the corners.

## Joe's Planting Tip

Try growing tomatoes in a Growing Bag that is cut in two across the middle. Then stand the sections on their ends. You have then got a deep root run in which to sustain the plants during the season.

When Growing Bags have been stacked for a while they go solid. A good idea to loosen them is to bang them on the ground. Alternatively, thump and then jiggle the bag to loosen and evenly disperse the compost. I call this 'Grow Bag Bashing'.

## Top Varieties

The best varieties I have grown in recent years are:

**Tumbler**
Excellent outdoor bush type.

**Britain's Breakfast**
Plum-shaped, sometimes as many as sixty per truss.

**Sun Baby**
Yellow fruit. Excellent flavour. Does well indoors or outside.

**Sunbelle**
Good indoors or out. Plum-shaped, small yellow fruits. Ideal in tubs or containers.

**Shirley**
Makes a good, strong plant. Still does well on the show bench. Good-shaped fruit, medium size.

**Golden Sunrise**
Excellent shape, very sweet.

**Gardeners Delight**
Very popular with my customers at the nursery. Wonderful flavour with a mixture of sweet and acid in the same bite. Large cherry type.

For people like myself who like to grow for exhibition, the varieties Classy and Cederico are now firm favourites. Have fun growing tomatoes. I look forward by early May to our first Tumblers F1 – a tried and trusted variety. I grow them indoors to get them early.

## Aftercare

Feed once a week with a tomato fertiliser. My method of feeding is to use a pelleted sheep manure, now called SlugGone. (www.sluggone.com). I scatter some sixty pellets around the top of the buckets. This is a slow release organic feed that will last the season.

Sheep manure is one of Charles Maisey's favourite ingredients for feeding his plants and Charles is one of our best amateur growers. These pellets will also deter slugs and snails.

## Tomatoes in the border soil:

The traditional way of growing tomatoes in the greenhouse is in the border soil. I recently went back to this method. I dug in some well-rotted compost in February and used one handful of SlugGone (pelleted sheep manure). Instead of supporting the plants by tying string around the bottom and onto a strand wire, which is the commercial method, I placed a cane to each plant. I then tied the plant to the cane. This way is safer because if the plants are supported only by string and it breaks, then you have a problem. Feed once a fortnight with tomato fertiliser and never allow the plants to get very dry.

## Double-stemmed Tomato

The double-stem method of growing has been very successful for me. I allow the main stem to develop and it is then trained up a lower sideshoot, thus forming a double-stemmed plant. By the time the plants reach six feet, five trusses have developed on each stem. You must feed regularly as the plant is carrying a heavy crop and will run out of energy if starved.

Give a tomato feed once the plants start to flower.

## Hanging Basket tomatoes

Another method of growing tomatoes is in a hanging basket. The variety Tumbler F1 is ideally suited for basket culture as it has a branching habit in the form of a small bush. When the fruits form they hang down the side of the basket. The fruits are small – slightly bigger than the cherry type. Their breeding is from Gardeners Delight, which has such a wonderful flavour. I place moss around the outside edge of the basket. I then use Growing Bag compost as the medium and feed with high potash feed every fourteen days. Keep well watered. The basket can be hung outside from late May to early June.

## Joe's Basket Tip

Try a few early-sown Tumbler tomatoes and grow on in the greenhouse. These will be ripe before traditional types.

# Cucumbers

Most amateur gardeners have great difficulty with this crop – and so do lots of professional gardeners. We tend to grow cucumbers in cold greenhouses. Yet early in the year in March and early April the night temperature is too cold. You really need the temperature during the night not to fall below 50F. My planting time for cucumbers in my cold greenhouse in North Yorkshire is the end of May.

## Propagation

I like to sow cucumbers on about May 1st. They need a night temperature of between 65F and 70F for germination. They can be sown in John Innes No 1 or a good multipurpose compost. The seed is sown individually in small pots.

Germination at 70F is about forty-eight hours. Sow the seeds on their side with the pointed edge downward. The theory behind this is that water drains away from the seed as if it was sown flat. Surplus moisture can rot the seeds. Cucumbers are also very prone to damping disease. I often think it necessary to pot on into five-inch pots. As the young plants grow on, use a small cane to keep them supported.

## Planting out

My best cucumbers have always been grown in my greenhouse borders on mounds of rotten strawy manure mixed with Growbag type material. I use one heaped barrowful of mixture to one plant. My fertiliser for all my crops is Sheep-it – one handful to each mound.

At planting time I make a hole in the mound and fill it with Growbag material. Knocking the plant out of the five-inch pot, I settle it into the mound. Now watch it grow – and at this stage do over-water. Distance between plants is a yard.

## Training

Train plants up long canes. My greenhouse eves are eight feet, so I take each plant up the cane. Tie in at regular intervals. As the plants are getting established, remove any young cucumbers. If you let them form they sap the strength of the plant, which makes it less productive later in growth. I also put spare canes a foot apart. If possible it is a good idea to attach canes to a strand wire for support.

As the plants grow on, they will start to produce side shoots. When young cucumbers form on these shoots, pinch out the growing point one leaf after the embryo cucumber. The extra canes placed in position are there to tie in the stopped side shoot bearing one cucumber. The tie will support it until it is large enough to eat.

## Removing cucumbers

I do not let cucumbers get too big before I harvest. Cutting them young encourages the plants to produce more cucumbers. One good plant should produce from mid-June to mid-September and give forty cucumbers per plant.

## Aftercare of growing plants

Cucumbers would love to be grown throughout their life at a temperature of 65F. Great fluctuations in temperature can produce a check and are especially prone to making the roots cold and wet. If followed by a high temperature the plant often droops and dies.

Cucumbers like it warm, but hot bright sunshine can also affect growth, so shading of the glass and careful ventilation should be practised.

## Varieties

Most people prefer to grow the types that are classed as all-female. This means the varieties do not produce male flowers. In open pollinated varieties like Telegraph, male flowers are formed. If one pollinates a female flower, the cucumber fills full of swollen seeds. It then tastes very bitter and is inedible. So varieties like Telegraph always require the male flowers removing, so pollination does not take place. The female types are F1 hybrids and are superior varieties, usually better flavour and more productive.

## F1 Carmen

Long smooth fruit that is bitter free with a high resistance to powdery mildew. It is all female

flowering. This is the best cucumber variety for exhibition work.

## F1 Femspot

Reliable variety suited to the conditions of a cool greenhouse.

## F1 Camilla

A very vigorous plant habit that shows good resistance to powdery mildew and is bitter free.

## F1 Passandra

A powdery mildew-resistant variety that is all-female and produces many small-sized fruits.

# Courgettes

## Ground preparation

Choose an area of the plot in an open sunny position to grow your courgettes. Set the garden line and place a cane at three-foot centres, then dig out a hole two feet square and fork through the base to combat poor drainage. Continue to dig the holes where you have placed the canes, then add one barrowful of well-rotted manure to each hole. If you cannot get manure, well-rotted garden compost or mushroom compost can be used instead.

When filling the hole filter in one forkful of manure then some soil then some manure and so on. Avoid a solid layer of manure as this can sometimes rot the roots. When you place the soil back onto the manure scatter in some slow-release sheep manure pellets. Pelleted chicken manure or Growmore could be used instead. By the time the manure and soil has gone back in the hole you have a mound approximately eighteen inches above soil level.

If you can, prepare your planting station six weeks before you want to plant out, this allows the soil to settle back with the manure and at planting time the moulds will be the correct degree of firmness. Don't forget to apply a general fertiliser to the adjacent areas around the planting area and fork in.

## Sowing your crop

I live in North Yorkshire and the correct sowing time in my area is at the end of April or early May. It takes me three to four weeks from sowing to having a plant at the stage to plant out, always bearing in mind that courgettes are on the tender side and do not like cold nights.

Courgette seed is quite large, so it is easy to handle. I like to sow my seeds into cell trays – fifteen cells per tray. Fill the trays using a good multi-purpose compost. Tap the full tray on the bench to firm in the compost and then water it well. Do not sow courgette seed flat, as sometimes water may lodge on the seed causing it to rot. Rather, sow the seed on its edge, pointed shape downwards so that the water runs away off it.

The seed trays can then be placed on a propagating mat or heated propagator, set at between 55-60F. Within five or six days, germination should have taken place. Remove the trays from the heat and grow on in the greenhouse, making sure they are in a warm, light position where the night temperature falls no lower than 40F. Ventilate well during the day.

Try to keep your plants sturdy, as courgettes grow very quickly. I transfer from the module trays to five-inch pots ten days after sowing. When the pots are full of roots and weather conditions permit, they can be planted. Put them in a well-ventilated cold frame prior to planting to harden them off thoroughly.

## Planting out

Water the plants well the night before planting. Make a depression twice the size of the root ball in the well prepared mounds, back fill and firm them in well before watering in.

Now the magic touch! To keep slugs at bay I like to make a circle around the plants using pelleted sheep manure (Slug Gone). The hygroscopic nature of the wool fibres in the pellets absorbs some of the slime underneath the slug's foot, drying it out and deterring it from crossing the barrier. When the barrier weathers it acts as slow-release plant food.

There is another ploy I use. As courgettes make big plants, fast-growing with a great leaf spread, it is impossible after a few weeks to gauge where to water. So I sink in a section of drainpipe about one foot away from the plant. I then know where the root system is located so I can water down the pipe. You could use a cut-down drinks bottle instead.

Courgettes love plenty of water in midsummer when they are producing well. If it becomes cold after planting, protect for a few days with cloches or even an upturned bucket at night.

An upturned bucket will protect newly planted courgettes on cold nights.

## Courgettes in containers and the greenhouse

To grow courgettes in a container it needs to be big enough – as big as a dustbin – and well drained. The same soil preparation is used as in the garden – one plant per bin. In a smaller container you may get a few courgettes but the plants do not thrive.

Many people try to grow courgettes in growing bags in the greenhouse. I often see three planted per bag, sometimes looking quite poorly. Fluctuations in temperature and lack of compost is the problem. Useful early crops can be grown in polytunnels but you will be fortunate if they last all summer long.

One of the questions frequently cropping up on my radio programmes is why do courgettes get to three-inches long and then go brown or drop off. This is often due to lack of fertilisation. On a courgette plant there are two types of flowers – male and female. The female flower has an embryo baby courgette attached at the rear, whereas the male

*Part 1. Vegetables*

Pick courgettes when they are small to avoid them turning into marrows.

### Joe's Harvesting Tip

To keep courgettes producing all summer and autumn, cut them when they are young. If a courgette reaches six inches in length remove it. If it is left to grow for a few more days it will develop into a marrow. It will then start to sap the strength of the plant, producing fewer courgettes as a result. Check your plants most days and remove regularly. Check the fruit every other day and harvest once it is about four to six inches long.

flower is normally smaller and does not have such an attachment. Lack of pollination or fertilization can be corrected by removing a male flower. When the female flower is fully open, brush pollen from the male to the female. During our summer months the job is nearly always completed by insects. When these are scarce, pollination can be poor. Try a plant on the patio in a large container.

### Favourite varieties

I have grown dozens of varieties in recent years. Here are some of the best:

### Ambassador
One of my best cropping varieties over the past ten years. Dark green fruit.

### Golden Zucchin F1
Very bright yellow courgettes, very strong grower, good flavour, cylindrical in shape.

### Defender F1
Crops earlier than any other variety sown at the same time. Attractive and one of the best on the show bench as they are easy to match. Good flavour too.

### Taxi F1
The heaviest cropping, yellow courgette I have grown. Good quality and easy to pick.

### Parthenon F1
A parthenoncarpic hybrid (does not require pollination by bees) and more suitable for protective growing in tunnel or greenhouse.

### Bambino F1
There is now a trend for using courgette flowers in cooking and many restaurants have deep-fried flowers on their menus. This variety can be harvested with the flower on or it can be detached. Very heavy yields of baby, dark green courgettes.

There are so many varieties available. Round varieties are delicious too – and ideal for stuffing.

# Aubergines

These have now become a popular greenhouse crop in summer. They require a good temperature and if they could be grown at a constant 64F they would love it. As this is difficult to achieve a constant watch must be kept on your ventilation systems, opening and closing doors to suit conditions.

## Seed sowing

Sow in a propagator in a heated greenhouse in early February at a temperature of 70F. Reduce to 65F after germination. Seed can be sown in a good multipurpose compost or John Innes seed compost.

## Potting

When the first seed leaves have straightened they can be moved on into three-inch pots, again using multipurpose compost or John Innes No 1. I like to water aubergines early in the day, which allows the compost to dry out before nightfall. Then the roots are not stood wet or cold overnight.

When the plants are growing strongly in May and have filled the small pots with roots, I put them into their final pots. In recent years I have had good results by using Growbag compost in twelve-inch pots. Once they are flowering, start feeding with tomato feed every ten days.

Your first fruits could be ready in July. Each plant may give six fruits.

Aubergines growing in the greenhouse.

# Pepper plants and Chillies

Twenty-five years ago peppers and chillies were hardly seen, but now most shopping centres will have these very popular items in them. I have noticed over the past ten years that most people buying tomato plants at my nursery will also take away four pepper and two chilly plants.

If you want to grow your own, sow in a propagator in February and proceed exactly as I have explained with aubergines. Instead of using twelve-inch pots I use florist buckets with drainage holes (see this chapter).

Start to feed after the first flowers have set. You should expect the first peppers in July. Each plant can produce about eight mature peppers or twelve to fourteen if eaten young. Chillies make a very ornamental plant, often handsome on the window sills. In smaller pots you need to feed every week with tomato feed.

*A Favourite Tale*

# The Largest Pumpkin

**A truly giant pumpkin!**

On the demonstration garden in Golden Acre Park we had a theme set up by Steve Mercer who worked for Which? magazine as Senior Researcher. The theme was to grow as many different vegetables of one genus each year. As already mentioned, the first year was a hundred varieties of onions and the following year we grew two hundred of potatoes. The third year we grew as many marrows and pumpkins as we could find!

At the time the world's largest pumpkin was a master weighing in at over 500 pounds grown by Howard Dill in Nova Scotia. He patented the seed known as Atlantic Giants so that people all over could grow these monster pumpkins.

So I set off to grow a big one using the variety Atlantic Giant. With pumpkins, it is important that you do not sow too early, as they don't like cold weather. I thought I would experiment, so they were sown at the end of February in a heated greenhouse. They were then transplanted into three-inch pots. By the end of March they were big plants in five-inch pots and by April they were huge plants in ten-inch pots! By early May they were getting enormous, like rhubarb with huge leaves, so I decided to plant them directly into a polythene tunnel.

I dug out a pit with approximately one barrowful of soil covering a yard, forked up at the bottom of the pit to allow good drainage. Next I wheeled in some well-rotted farm yard manure and used a product new to me called 'Dags'. (See the 'Sheep-it' story at the end of this chapter.) The sheep manure pellets were applied with about a handful to each square yard that had been dug out. Then, the large plant was placed in the centre of the pit to enable it to get the warmth of the polythene cover.

The pumpkin plants soon took over the area, growing extremely quickly, and I had flowers by early June. It is necessary for the plant to have male and female flowers open at the same time so that pollination can take place. The female flowers have a baby pumpkin all ready to grow once fertilisation occurs. One morning in mid-June, I went to look at the plants and one had formed a pumpkin the size of an apple. The following week it was as big as a football, and three weeks later it was as big as a car tyre! It just kept on growing. Visitors to Golden Acre Park's demonstration area were able to admire it growing in the corner of the poly tunnel next to a main path. There was a tap close by and every day it was given fifteen minutes of water from the hosepipe.

One day in early September, the Lord Mayor of Leeds, Councillor Denise Atkinson, visited the park. She said to me, "What are you going to do with that?"

I thought quickly and said, "You can have it for your charity if you like." My idea was to get it down to the Leeds Civic Hall and have it on display. Visitors would be charged £1 to guess the weight and the funds would go to help swell the Lord Mayor's Charity Box.

Along with Alistair Muir, who worked for the Parks Department and helped to grow the giant, I set out one day to cut the pumpkin from the plant and try and get it into my car. What a weight it was! We puffed and pouted and got it stuck between the car door and the steering wheel. Eventually we just about got it seated in the front seat, overflowing and touching the handbrake. I strapped it in with the car safety belt and set off down to Leeds Civic Hall. As I was driving past Headingley Cricket Ground, I soon realised that Yorkshire had just lost the match. A supporter came to the car window whilst the traffic lights were on red and said, "He could 'ave done better than that lot in there", pointing to the pumpkin sat in the front seat!

Down at Leeds Civic Hall, they had sent two chaps and a trolley out to help. They soon went back in for two more chaps and we all lifted it inside and put it into position at the entrance to the ballroom. It stayed there for some three weeks and raised over £700. The day of the weighing finally arrived and John Tinker, then Director of the Parks, had brought his balancing scales made from an old seesaw. We sat the Lord Mayor on one end of the platform and the pumpkin on the other and the final weight was 225 pounds! But that wasn't the last of the pumpkin.

On the day of Halloween, me and my son John, who would have been about twelve at the time, carved a face into the giant pumpkin. As we hollowed it out we removed all the seeds and dried them. Then we sold them for £1 a packet to go in the fund. The pumpkin made its final journey to a children's home for a party. The last I heard was that it was on its way up to a moon after a firework blew it up! But really that was not the end of it, as I sowed twenty large seeds myself and this strain is still the one that features in Grow with Joe's seed catalogue. The seeds from the best pumpkins are saved, dried, packed and the variety is 'Atlantic Giant type Own Saved'.

Mixed salad leaves growing in containers.

# Salad Leaves

For the perfect salad there is no substitute for freshness. It is wonderful to be able to go into the garden, pick fresh salad leaves and then wash, prepare and eat them within the hour. Money cannot buy this experience and salad crops are so easy to produce. Most crops grow well on land well-manured for a previous crop with added fertiliser like blood, fish and bone meal.

We are living at a time when things are easy for us. A visit to a supermarket can produce a bag of mixed salad leaves and a quick and easy meal, but once the bag has been opened the freshness starts to decrease rapidly. A lot of the following leaf vegetables in this section can be found in salad packs.

### Pak Choi Red and  Pak Choi Toi Choi

Wonderful in fresh salads. Quick growing summer long but frost susceptible. Can be sown in drills or broadcast half an inch deep. When the leaves are usable size after six to eight weeks, break them off so the plant continues to grow. Best picked fresh, as Pak Choi does not store well. Last sowing in the autumn, say eight weeks before the first frosts are expected.

### Tatsoi Pak Choi

Good stand-by winter greens in frames or cold greenhouse. Dark spoon-shaped leaves. You can cut the complete plant, leaving an area of stem which will re-grow for further cutting. Tatsoi has the problem of bolting if it lacks moisture in its early stages.

### Corn salad

Often called Lambs Lettuce. Variety – Jade. Sow outdoors from April to August, half an inch deep into prepared damp soil. This is a crop that succeeds well as a cut-and-come again. Very early sowings need making under cloches. For a continuous crop sow every three to four weeks and take a few leaves each time. For larger more mature leaves, space plants six inches apart. Corn salad can be grown in pots in the greenhouse, sowing in September for use through the winter. It is best picked fresh.

A wonderful supper dish is cold pheasant on a bed of corn salad with a glass of red wine and some nice fresh crusty bread.

### Beet – Bulls Blood

Very dark red beetroot leaf wonderful to add colour to salads. When picked young, always leave a few leaves, as colour does intensify as plants mature. Soil must be moist but do not over-water. We used this with silver cineraria in the Parks Department as a border-edging plant.

### Perilla

Other plants we used in bedding displays in the Parks Department were the red and green types of perilla to give height in the centre of beds. Perilla can be used in salads or to season fish. It is best sown in gentle heat in a greenhouse, pricked on into module trays or small pots and planted out when the frost has gone. It is a good idea to pinch out the growing point to make bushy plants, as then you can pick the leaves and use fresh as required.

### Amaranth red

You can sow Amaranth outdoors in spring to late summer. I think it is best to sow thinly in rows and thin seedlings to two inches apart. If you require large plants, thin to ten inches apart. The young leaves are produced quickly and can be used in salads after about four weeks. The leaves gain a more intense red as they develop.

# Lettuce

The basic for most people's salads is of course the humble lettuce. By using various varieties we can be eating fresh lettuce leaves all the year round. For many months we can also have wonderful crispy and crunchy lettuce hearts.

*Lettuce types:*

### Butterheads
Flattish rounded heads, soft texture.

### Cos Little Gem Romaine
Tall and upright.

*Loose heart-forming, both large and small types:*

### Crisp Iceberg type
Crisp leaves, crisp and compact hearts.

### Batavian
Thinner leaves than Iceberg; thicker and crisper leaves than Butterheads.

### Loose leaf, Curled leaf and Oak leaf types
These are mainly non-hearting types. A wide range of colours and leaf textures, often called cut-and-come again. Pick the leaves over long periods.

### Lollo Rossa types
Non-hearting, often curled in centres with lots of curled leaves.

The following varieties should give you fresh lettuces throughout the year. Just think of fresh home-grown lettuce at Christmas time with all the cold meats. You can go and pick it from the greenhouse the day you require it and not have to try and keep it fresh, knowing it must have been picked well in advance in order to get it in the shops in time.

### Wymona

Can be sown in August, grown as cool as possible in modules or pots, and planted in September in a cold greenhouse. Butterhead type to pick through the winter. It can be sown up to February but requires the protection of cold frames or cloches.

### Valdor and Parella green

Also very good varieties for protective growth when sowing lettuce seed in summer time. Try and find a cool place to germinate the seed. It was always said that lettuce seeds go into dormancy when the temperature gets above 75 Fahrenheit.

### Winter Imperial, Arctic King and Winter Density

All hardy winter outdoor types from autumn sowings to be ready in springtime. Can be brought on early by using cloches. Winter lettuces can be grown very close together. Can be thinned out and used as baby rosette-forming hearts, giving room for the other plants to develop to full size.

### Trocadero

An old variety that can be sown in autumn or in spring. Very good from February through till May. Butterhead type.

### Little Gem Cos type, Susan Butterhead type and Lobjoits Green Cos.

These are really old favourites. I start to make sowings in late February or March. Sowing can be made in July for hearted lettuces from May till October.

### Salad Bowl and Red Salad Bowl

I make a sowing in early February. My last sowing is made in August. In mild years it is possible to pick leaves well into the winter. I have been successful with fresh leaves through the winter in pots and containers in the cold greenhouse.

Iceberg type of lettuce.

Winter Density lettuce outside in February tucked into a Link-a-Bord raised bed.

*Part 1. Vegetables*

# Sheep-it

Thirty years ago my spot on Radio Leeds went on air at 7am on Saturday mornings and was called Gardeners' Direct Line, which followed on from the TV series with Geoffrey Smith and Peter Seabrook. When this TV series finished, it seemed a good idea to put it on local radio. The radio programmes would be aired with different people and there would be a chairman in charge. Questions came in via the telephone and we gardeners would answer the listener's problems. People would also send in queries such as identifying plants and topics to discuss. We thought that a lot of people's days started at seven with a cup of tea and Gardeners' Direct Line.

One Saturday morning some thirty years ago, with Andy Joyson in the chair at two minutes to seven, he handed me a package and asked me to look at it. He said we would later discuss it live on air. I was looking at the package and reading the information on the label as the programme started and as Andy did the introduction. Then he said to me, "Joe, what is in that package I handed you?"

I began to read out the package over the airwaves and the name on it said 'Dags'. Underneath this it said, 'By product from the wool industry, totally odourless.' Then on the front there was a photograph of a sheep. The package had been sent in by the manufacturers. Suddenly, I realised what I had in front of me – it was a bag of sheep shit! Andy was not aware of the contents of the bag and he was quite an impatient young man in those days. He kept saying, "Tell us all about the package Joe."

So I began to share the contents of the package with the listeners. I thought the best way was to split the bag open and to my surprise it ponged! The package had said totally odourless but it had been living in Radio Leeds for a week by the side of a radiator. It had gone off a little bit creating a stench.

Andy persisted in asking what it was, so I put some of the contents of the bag into the palm of his hand and told him to give it a good smell. It was in fact dry, flaky bits of sheep droppings with the wool attached and it really blew his hat off! The listeners started ringing in with their favourite recipes for sheep manure. Donald from Skelmanthorpe called it Doddlings, which he soaked in water and then put on his plants.

I remember my dad sending us into the field in front of our house – 'us' being Berny Elliot and myself. Berny was known locally as Bunny. We used to collect the sheep droppings and put them in a bucket. When Bunny wasn't looking I used to slip a few into his pocket. I bet his mum gave him what for when he got home! Dad would then transfer the droppings to a hessian sack and dangle it into a 45 gallon drum of water leaving an old brush handle close by. He would use this to stir the contents – what a smell! The mixture could boast bluebottles as big as blackbirds and dad used it to feed all the plants in the garden. He would put one pint to two gallons of water and it came out looking like a weak tea colour.

Back on the radio when we finished on the theme of sheep manure, the programme ran as normal. On the Monday morning after the show I received a phone call from a representative of the manufacturers. He told me they had received many enquiries after the show and he asked me if I wanted to sample some for my garden. I told him I would be delighted and he sent me twenty bags. At the time it was in half hundredweight polythene bags and it felt quite light, but with condensation the moisture content increased and the bags started to cause an odour problem. The material, Dags as it was then called, was fantastic. We did some simple trials such as feeding half a row with it and leaving the other half without feed – and the results were amazing. You have to see it to believe it and to this day it is the only base fertiliser I use. The best part is that it is totally organic.

For the company to manufacture Dags for sale, a big change had to take place. Dags consisted of dry, flaky bits of sheep manure with the wool attached, but it was soon developed into pellet form and this was a remarkable change. I think it is the best product in horticulture and I use it for all my growing on the nursery – hanging baskets, tomatoes, shrubs, fruit trees, roses, perennials and so on. Each pellet is about the size of a hen's laying pellet and has wool fibre and

I regularly use Sheep-it, also sold as Slug Gone, for top-dressing.

sheep manure squashed into it. As it starts to degrade in the soil with the moisture, plants immediately begin to feed and then the pellet rots down further as the wool and fibre content is slower to decompose. This gives the product a slow-release action and so plants are fed organically over a very long period of time.

If three or four small pellets are put onto an old spoon and dampened with water, within a few minutes they will have trebled in size and filled the spoon. Therefore in dry weather conditions this amazing product will help to conserve water.

When I use the product in hanging baskets, I put about thirty pellets to a basket and this will feed it for the whole season. The root hairs feed on the rotting wool fibres late season and keep the plants in good condition.

The new name for Dags is Sheep-it and we now have this product made for us. My son John wanted to use an old fashioned name, Sheep Shit, but we decided to keep the 'sh' out of it and so it is Sheep-it.

One evening I was giving a talk in Barnsley and I took some Sheep-it with me. The chairman brought me a pint of beer over and this was plonked on my demonstration table. I opened up a packet of Sheep-it and started to extol its virtues. I said, "If you have a house plant indoors, all you need to do is make a hole with a pencil down the side of the plant and slip a couple of pellets in."

As I was talking I was also feeding the plants at the table when I noticed something floating in my beer. I realised it was a pellet and with the fizz of the beer it started to propel itself around the glass, went to the bottom and then surfaced. I thought there was no way I was going to drink the beer, so I kept watching the chairman and when he wasn't looking I was going to tip it onto a pot of Hostas.

Later that evening, as the talk went on, I developed a bit of a cough. Forgetting all about the pellet, I took one long swig of beer and swallowed the lot! It is obviously totally safe and completely organic, as I am still here. But remember it's sheep shit so don't eat it!

*Part 1. Vegetables*

# Vegetable Questions and Answers

### 1. What causes potato scab?
This is a microorganism that lives in the soil. If the soil is of a limey or gritty nature, the irritation induces wart-like growths on the skin known as potato scab.

### 2. Why do my potatoes go rotten in the soil?
Often this occurs due to potato blight – a fungal disorder, it first appears on the foliage. The spores are washed into the soil by rain or water, which causes the potatoes to rot. This disease is worst when we get humid conditions in July.

### 3. How do we control potato blight?
By spraying with a systemic fungicide or using blight-resistant varieties such as Lady Balfour, Milva and Orla.

### 4. Is it right to remove potato flowers?
By removing the flowers the energy that goes into them is best employed by bulking up the crop of potatoes.

### 5. Why do lots of little holes appear in my potatoes?
The holes are often caused by the keeled slug. This tiny black slug lives under the ground and eats into the flesh of the potatoes causing holes and channels.

### 6. What does 'chitting' potatoes mean?
Potato sets are often put into a light place in early spring in order to form little hard shoots that grow from the eyes. This is the process called 'chitting'.

'Chitting' – the process that causes shoots to grow from the eyes of potatoes.

### 7. Can I grow Jersey Royals in Yorkshire?
These potatoes have been given this name because they are grown on the island of Jersey. Yet there is no variety known as Jersey Royal. The variety is International Kidney. It grows extremely well in Yorkshire and can be used prematurely as a baby new potato. But when left to mature naturally it is a large kidney potato.

### 8. Why do I always fail with carrots because of a maggot?
The maggot is the larvae of the carrot fly. Spray regularly with Garlic Wonder (see question 17). The smell of the garlic masks that of the carrot foliage. I find this a very successful method.

Removing potato flowers to help bulk up the crop.

**9. Can I grow carrots in pots?**

Carrots can be grown very successfully in deep pots using a sandy compost. A sowing made in August and brought through the winter in a cold greenhouse will be ready for use as baby carrots from Christmas time until Easter. The variety is Amsterdam Forcing. They can also be grown in deep pots in summer time.

**10. When do I sow parsnips?**

Parsnips are one of the first vegetable seeds that can be sown out into the vegetable garden. Normally ground preparation is done during the winter months by deeply digging the soil. Like all root vegetables, parsnips are grown on land that has been well manured for a previous crop. In Yorkshire if the ground conditions permit, I like to sow parsnip seed about the second week in March, but I have also had great success by sowing in April.

**11. Why should you not cut the tops off beetroot?**

There is a tendency for beetroot to lose its colour if the tops are cut off. It is best to twist the tops.

**12. Can I grow a crop of French Beans in pots in the greenhouse to get them early?**

Yes – I do this every year. Varieties like Prince are ideal. Sow in March and they can be ready in May.

**13. I had some pea shoots in a restaurant. Are they easy to grow as they were delicious as a starter?**

Very easy and it only takes three weeks maximum in a greenhouse in shallow trays. Pull out, remove roots, wash and eat.

**14. How do I save Broad Bean seed?**

Only save from plants that have cropped well. Leave pods on plants till they go black, then shell and thoroughly dry the seed. Put in packets ready for sowing next season.

Beetroot tops should be twisted rather than cut off.

Arching the leaves over a cauliflower helps to maintain their beautiful white texture.

**15 My cauliflowers go yellow. How do I keep them white?**

Many books will tell you that when the small cauliflower in the base of the plant is developing, it is necessary to bend some leaves over it in order to keep out the light. But on a sunny day the leaves wilt and the light gets in, making the developing cauliflower go yellow. With a piece of string, tie the leaves and arch them above the embryo cauliflower. This keeps out the light, maintaining a beautiful white cauliflower.

### 16. We always fail with cauliflowers. Is there a reason?

Many people fail with cauliflowers because their land is not good enough. They like a rich soil on the heavy side with plenty of lime. There is a variety of cauliflower for every month of the year. In general terms, cauliflowers take between 90 and 120 days for maturing from sowing the seed.

### 17. How do I stop Cabbage White butterfly caterpillars on all my brassicas?

In recent years a spray containing garlic and called Garlic Wonder has been developed. It is very effective as a barrier against butterflies. They will not lay their eggs when they smell the garlic. Spray once every fortnight as a fine mist when butterflies are seen. It also acts as a folio feed.

### 18. I love coleslaw in winter. What is the best variety of cabbage?

The best cabbages for making coleslaw are an F1 hybrid called Bartola and the F1 variety called Impala. They make very little internal core.

Wellington is one of the varieties of Brussels Sprouts that can produce firm buttons.

### 19. My Brussels Sprouts are always loose forming. Why?

To get firm buttons on your Brussels Sprouts plants they need to be on good land and firmed in well after planting. Modern varieties like F1 Diablo, F1 Bosworth and F1 Wellington produce very firm buttons.

### 20. When do I sow chard seed?

Chard seed is best sown during May, June and July – any earlier and it may go to seed. Chard is now a very popular over-wintering vegetable that does well in the spring prior to going to seed in May.

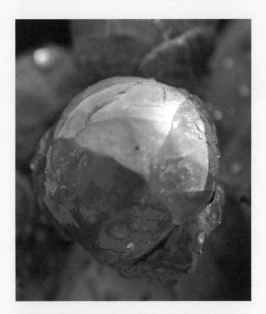

Peeling off the weathered leaves of cabbages exposes the solid white heart, which is ideal for making coleslaw.

Chard is a wonderful over-wintering vegetable that does well in the spring.

Bright Lights, with its large range of colours, is an extremely useful mixture of chard.

### 21. What are the best varieties of chard?

An extremely useful mixture is Bright Lights with its large range of colours – white, cream, yellow, orange, pink and red. Other recommended varieties include Flamingo and Canary Yellow.

### 22. Can I grow spinach in winter time?

Yes – the variety Palco is good, as is Giant Winter. Sow in August and September.

### 23. Our spinach goes to seed within weeks of sowing. What is the best variety to sow in summer?

Bella F1 is slow to bolt. Bloomsdale has masses of leaves and unlike other varieties is slow to go to seed in hot weather.

### 24. I would love to grow a Giant Onion. What seed do I use ?

The best variety is Kelsae.

### 25. Why do my onion sets go to seed?

This happens when there has been a check in the growth due to cold wet weather.

Palco is a superb variety of spinach with its thick and fleshy leaves suited to autumn, winter and spring production.

### 26. Can shallots be grown from seed?

Yes – seed can be sown direct into shallow drills in good soil. Each seed grows a single shallot. Matador is a good variety.

### 27. Can I grow Baby Leeks in containers?

Yes – use good compost and sow sixty seeds to a florist's bucket with drainage holes in the base. Use the variety Jolant.

The bases of marrows can often rot if they are not separated from the soil .

Ideal is one of the old-fashioned varieties of celery that will keep growing into November.

**28. I once saw some large leeks at a show that had been grown from pips. What are pips?**
Pips are taken from the flowerhead of the leek in its second year.

**29. How do I grow tomatoes from cuttings?**
Easy – take off a side shoot about four inches long and put it in a jar of water on a window sill. It will root in about ten days. Place in a small pot of compost. You will have plants in no time!

**30. Which is the best cucumber for growing outdoors?**
In my North Yorkshire garden I find Market More and F1 Burpless tasty green do very well.

**31. When do I sow Sweet Corn in Yorkshire?**
Inside in late April. Harden off to plant outside at the end of May.

**32. What is the best variety for growing in the North?**
Sweet Nugget grows extremely well in my Yorkshire garden. It performs very well in cooler conditions.

**33. Why do people put glass or slate under marrows?**
This is done to stop soil marking and rotting the base of the marrows.

**34. How do I grow the old fashioned type of celery?**
Sow in February and plant out in good rich soil in May after growing-on in pots in a cold frame. The varieties Ideal, Pascal and Giant Red need blanching but will keep growing well into November. They have an excellent texture and nutty flavour.

**35. What does it mean by 'blanching' celery?**
This means drawing up the soil round the stems to keep out light and thus causing them to go tender. Showmen often use either corrugated cardboard or black dampcourse material tied round the stems.

**36. How do I grow Giant Pumpkin?**
The best variety is Atlantic Giant. Plenty of manure needs to be added to the soil, followed by lots of water and liquid fertiliser.

A glorious array of early spring vegetables ready in February.

**37. I want to construct some raised beds. What is the best depth and size?**
Anything up to eighteen inches deep and four feet wide.

**38. What is the best material for making raised beds?**
I have used Link-a-Bord raised beds for years. They are attractive, easy to assemble and vegetables grow very well in them.

**39. Can I do crop rotation on raised beds?**
We try our best but it is difficult. Try not to grow the same crop in the same place the following year.

**40. What vegetables can I grow to either store or have fresh in February and March?**
All the vegetables shown in the photograph on this page, plus carrots, parsnips, sprouting broccoli, winter spinach, leeks and winter lettuce.

*Part 1. Vegetables*

Fresh fruit picked on a summer's day is always a glorious sight.

# PART 2. FRUIT AND HERBS

I could write a whole book about fruit. Fresh fruit picked and eaten when ripe on an early summer's day in Yorkshire is one of the delights of my life. And not only on a summer's day because fruit can be produced up to late autumn, and certain apples and pears can be stored and eaten well into late spring using certain varieties.

Before I start pontificating about this very important section, I have to refer to a statement from the Royal Horticultural Society's handbook that claims rhubarb is a vegetable. My wife, who is a Yorkshire lass from Pudsey, was brought up in the rhubarb-growing area of the county. Rhubarb was used in pies and with custard as a pudding. In Betty's eyes it is therefore a fruit and I am not disagreeing with her. My mum would also agree with Betty if she had still been with us.

## *Top Fruit*

Top Fruit is tree fruit – apples, pears, plums, damsons, cherries and so on. In my previous house garden I planted fruit trees. When we moved house they were just getting established. Good fruit trees are not cheap and I was reluctant to leave them. However, they were on the point of bearing fruit so they were left to grow on for the benefit of the next occupants.

Our new home had the great advantage of thirty established fruit trees – a bit neglected but they were there. It took me three years of pruning, spraying and feeding to bring them back. Now every year I look forward to the spring blossom followed by embryo fruit developing through the season into a good crop. This is one of the most satisfying aspects of gardening.

I would make one of my special statements: "If every gardener planted a fruit tree in their life many people would greatly benefit." Fruit trees are wonderful, giving blossom in the spring and fresh fruit from mid-summer to late autumn. Certain varieties permit fruit to be stored through the winter.

### Pollination and rootstocks

In most areas of the country the close proximity of other gardens provides good pollen. Due to the generous visits of bees and other insects, pollination is therefore successful. If a variety is triploid, it means that different varieties should be planted together in order to be compatible.

These days most varieties of plums are self-fertile

Fruit trees that had been neglected for twenty-five years are now fit again and in full production.

but cherries are a bit different. All fruit catalogues list the best varieties that are compatible with one another.

Rootstocks mainly have number codes. Details are given under each fruit.

### Soil condition

Fruit trees will not tolerate waterlogged or badly drained conditions. They need a sunny position and rainfall of between 20 and 25 inches per year. Prepare a planting hole by digging out a barrowful of soil. Mix in some old manure or compost. Backfill with the good soil and manure mix. Remember the old saying, 'If the tree costs £20 put it in a £30 hole.' When backfilling remove any stones, weeds and firm the tree in the well.

# Apples

## Planting – bare-rooted trees

These are trees that have been grown by specialist growers and lifted in October, when the leaves have dropped. They should be planted between October and March. The depth should be a fraction deeper then than the soil mark of the original planting. This is always stained just above the root area with soil.

## Planting – container-grown trees

These trees can be planted at any time of the year as they have been grown in containers with very little root disturbance. The main criteria is that you must water frequently even if it rains. Water will not often penetrate the dense root system in the rootball. It means that the plant can be stressed and can often die through lack of water. This applies until new roots get growing into your own soil.

Discovery variety of apples growing well in early July.

## Manuring

Make sure planting stations are well prepared. Apply one ounce per square yard of sulphate of ammonia in February or March, and one ounce of sulphate of potash. Two ounces of super phosphate of lime should be applied every three years.

## Pruning

Try and maintain an open-centred tree. Lightly tip the main leading shoots to about half their length. Later the leading shoots can be left unpruned. Remove crossing branches. Prune out dead and diseased wood or any very awkwardly placed branches.

## Harvesting

Eating or dessert apples should be gathered when they are ready to leave the tree when touched. Store in an airy and cool place out of the frost.

## Varieties – Eating Apples

Taste is a personal preference. Here are some of my favourites:

**Beauty of Bath:** Early August. Wonderful to eat straight off the tree.

**Discovery:** August and September. White flesh and very crisp, firm and juicy.

Container-grown trees on the nursery in July.

**Worcester Pearmain:** September and October, Wonderful apple that can be eaten from the tree in August. Crimson in colour.

**Sunset:** Use from October to Christmas. Golden fruits splashed with red. Magnificent when in flower, very reliable.

**Red Devil:** Dessert type. Use October to January. Very fruity taste. Wonderful red apple.

## Cooking Apples

**Bramley's Seedling:** Ready November till May. The best known of all culinary apples. Very large.

**Charles Ross:** Dual purpose – pick in September.

**Dog's Snout:** One of Yorkshire's rare varieties. Has its strange name because it resembles a dog's nose .Very hardy and reliable cropper.

**Howgate Wonder:** The largest of all cooking apples. Firm flesh and juicy – cooks well. Pick November. Ready December to February.

## Rootstocks

**M.27:** Very dwarf. Produces the true mini tree, reaching no more than two metres with little support required. Excellent for the small garden.

**M.9:** Dwarf. Very productive but poor anchorage, needing permanent staking for support. Ideal for cordons.

**M.26:** Semi-dwarf. Requires support on most sites. Good for bush and cordon in limited spaces.

**MM.106:** Semi-vigorous. General purpose for most types of cordon and half standard. Staking only required on sites that are exposed.

**MM.111:** Vigorous. As for MM.106 but more ideal for half standards. No staking required. Excellent collar rot and general disease resistance.

**M.25:** Very Vigorous. Ideal for half and full standards.

# Pears

Cultivation and manuring are similar to apples. Plenty of compost should be applied as a mulch in spring, but should be forked into the soil the following autumn. Nitrogen is needed when plenty of blossom has been produced but little extension growth. The best fertiliser is three-quarters of an ounce of nitro chalk to the square yard. Apply half an ounce of sulphate of potash to the square yard in early spring.

## Varieties

**Conference:** Ready October and November. The favourite pear in Yorkshire. Well flavoured and very juicy when ripe.

**Doyenne du Comice:** Ready November and December. Known to be the finest pear for flavour. Likes a warm and sheltered site.

**Onward:** Pick and use in September. Wonderful pear – its only downfall is a short season of use.

**Pear Catillac:** Pick September and will store until April. The best of all the culinary types.

## Rootstocks

**Quince 'C':** Dwarf and slightly earlier into cropping.

**Quince 'A':** Semii-dwarf. The ideal root stock for bush trees.

**Pyrodwarf:** Vigorous. Specifically for perry varieties but useful for all pears. A robust tree with early fruiting.

**Pyrus communis:** Very vigorous. More suitable for half standard and especially standard trees.

Victoria plums forming in early July.

# Plums

### Cultivation

Plums like well cultivated ground, but are quite happy in most soils. They must not be grown in waterlogged conditions but will do very well on heavy land. Like all stone fruit they enjoy lime. They are best grown as a half standard with say five feet of clear stem before branching

### Pruning.

Little pruning is necessary once the framework of branches has been formed. This is normally done before the tree has been purchased. Any pruning such as diseased wood, or broken or overcrowded branches, is normally done in summer time. The cuts heal quickly, so summer pruning helps to curb the plum disease called silver leaf as it is more active in late autumn and winter.

### Varieties

**Early Laxton:** Ready in July. Culinary or dessert type.

**Czar:** Early August – a culinary type.

**Victoria:** Late August. The best-loved plum, which does fantastically in my Yorkshire garden. It is self-fertile but is a good pollinator of all other varieties.

**Warwickshire Drooper:** Late September, self-fertile. Can be used for cooking or as a lovely dessert type.

### Rootstocks

**Pixy:** Dwarf and ideal for size containment in the garden.

**St Julien 'A':** Semi-vigorous. Fully compatible with all plums, damsons, gages, peaches, nectarines, apricots and many ornamental prunus species.

**Brompton:** Vigorous, suitable for standards.

# Damsons

The cultivation and treatment of damsons is similar to that of plums. One good thing about the tough old damson is that it can form good shelter belt for other subjects because of its twiggy growth.

### Varieties

**Farleigh:** Ready mid-September.

**Merry Weather:** Ready September and October.

**Shropshire Prune:** Ready mid-September.

# Cherries (Sweet)

Cherry Bigarreau Napoleon – noted for its pale yellow fruits that are delicious straight off the tree.

## Cultivation

The ideal place to grow cherries is a light loam on well-drained chalky subsoil. Cherries flower in the early spring, so an area not in a frost pocket will be ideal. They eventually make a large tree so it is important to give them space. Cherry trees require very little feeding once they get established. Two ounces of bonemeal and a light dressing of sulphate of ammonia in spring should be ideal for each tree.

## Pruning

Sweet cherries require little or no pruning apart from the removal of dead, diseased, damaged or unwanted wood.

## Varieties

**Early Rivers:** Early red cherry, very sweet.

**Cherry Stella:** Pick July and August. Self-fertile cherry with dark red fruits that have a very good flavour.

**Cherry Bigarreau Napoleon:** Pale yellow fruits delicious straight off the tree. This variety needs a pollinator.

**Cherokee:** Used all July and August. Self-fertile. Large crops of luscious dark red fruit.

## Rootstocks

**Colt:** Semi-vigorous. Very productive and fully compatible with all sweet and flowering varieties. Will contain trees to 4 to 5 metres.

**Gisela 5:** Dwarf, 60 per cent of Colt. Ideal for commercial orchards, garden, and patio pots.

**Prunus F.12.1:** Very vigorous.

# Cherries (Acid)

Acid types are generally used for culinary purposes. The best varieties are:

**Morello:** Ready in August – ideal for stewing. If left to go black it becomes much sweeter.

**Kentish Red:** Another cherry for stewing, etc.

# Questions and Answers

*1. I have terrible trouble keeping pests and diseases off my fruit trees. Is there a magic potion?*
Yes I think I have found one. They call it Garlic Wonder fruit tree care. This can be used frequently during winter, spring and summer. The natural sulphur in garlic acts as a fungicide, which helps to build up the resistance against fungal disorders. It also acts as a folio feed making the leaves stronger to withstand any insect attack. I also think the smell of the garlic keeps insects at bay.

*2. My plum tree is constantly carrying a tremendous heavy crop resulting in branches being broken by the sheer weight of the crop. How do I stop this happening?*
By cutting some fork-shaped branches in winter time – usually from ash saplings – and store these until they are needed. I then support the branches by using them underneath the weight of the crop.

*3. What is a family tree?*
Three or five varieties grafted on the same tree. It means you can grow different types of eating and cooking apples that will pollinate each other.

*4. What are Cordon trees?*
Single-stem tree planted 2ft 6 in apart at an angle of 45 degrees, and normally trained on wires. All the natural growths are kept trimmed back.

*5. What is an Espalier tree?*
A tree where the branches are trained horizontally from the trunk.

*6. What is a Pyramid tree?*
A bush-type tree with a little trunk. Branches are kept conveniently low for ease of picking and spraying. It is good for the smaller garden.

*7. My Cox Orange Pippin only fruits once in seven years in our North Yorkshire village. Why?*
Cox Orange Pippins are not the best to grow in the North of England. A good substitute is the variety called Sunset.

*8. What is the best eating apple for a small garden?*
Epicure is an excellent variety, resistant to frost and with a very compact habit. It is my number one for a small garden.

*9. Is there a Russet variety of apple that is self-fertile and suitable for the North of England?*
In my garden I have Egremont Russet, which fruits every year. I pick it in October and we always have beautiful apples at Christmas time.

*10. I have been told that crab apple trees are good to pollinate other varieties. Is this true?*
Yes – Golden Gem, Red Sentinel and Golden Hornet are excellent small garden trees, fantastic when in flower and wonderful for small gardens – as well as making crab apple jelly.

*11. What is Silver Leaf?*
It is the worst disease that members of the plum family can get. It is a fungus disease, whereby the spores enter the trees through pruning cuts or broken branches in winter time. It is best to prune in the summer time so that all the cut areas heal over quickly and the infection cannot get into the sap stream.

*12. Can new damson trees be grown from suckers?*
Most varieties of damson trees can be grown successfully form basal suckers.

*13. Can you name a variety of peach tree to go on a small south-facing garage wall?*
Peregrine is very hardy and self-fertile and probably the best variety for the small garden.

*14. Can apricots be grown in the North of England?*
They need a sheltered position near to a south-facing wall. The soil has to be well drained with a high lime content.

*15. Do peaches, apricots and nectarines need other trees to pollinate them?*
No – all the varieties are self-fertile.

Branches can be broken by the sheer weight of a crop.

## Soft Fruit

# Strawberries

It is extremely important to grow strawberries to their full potential and it is best to get nothing but the best stock. This is obtainable from growers who have been given a DEFRA Certificate A Grade for their stock. They will be able to quote the number and the certificate should guarantee the stock is fit, healthy and free from virus disease.

### Site

It is said that strawberries are woodland plants. I feel a site that can provide as much sunshine as possible, south facing and on a slight slope would be the ideal. Try to avoid a site that is subject to wet and cold weather, which could check the growth and inhibit the crop.

### Soil condition and preparation

Strawberries love to be grown on land that has been dug deeply with plenty of well-rotted old farmyard manure incorporated and mixed through the soil, although not in deep layers. The soil should be well drained yet should retain its moisture well in dry weather conditions. I had a fantastic strawberry bed that was prepared by digging in lots of well-rotted beach leaf mould.

### Planting

In order to get an early crop the young plants should be planted in July and August. They should give a small crop, often of excellent quality, in their first year. The planting distance between each row should be 2ft 6in with 18 inches between the plants. Take out a planting hole with a trowel large enough to accommodate the roots without bending. The planting depth should be sufficiently deep so the crown of the plant sits just above soil level.

If the crown is too high the roots tend to dry and shrivel causing the plant to die. If planted too deep it could cause the plant to rot away. Make sure when planting that you firm in well.

In the first few months, as the plant is getting established, keep the roots moist. In early spring apply a dressing of two ounces to the yard run of row of sulphate of ammonia, an ounce of sulphate of potash and two ounces of super phosphate. Keep the fertiliser off the leaves but gently hoe into the soil.

### Fruiting

It was always said that in the first year you should remove the blossom in order to build up the plants. In recent times the vigour in the modern varieties has developed, so early crops can be achieved without damage to the plants.

The other day I had a question on my radio show. The lady said, "Joe, my strawberries are not as good as they used to be." I asked the question, "How long have they been planted?" She replied, "They were in the garden when we moved in twenty five years ago!" Strawberries should be discarded after four years, so each year put in some new plants and discard and remove the old ones.

### Protection from weather and birds

Strawberries form in trusses. Before the largest of the ripening berries weigh down the rest of the crop onto the soil, it is a good idea to put down a bed of straw. This will prevent soil being splashed onto the berries.

At this stage it is important to protect the strawberry crop from birds, which are very attracted to ripe berries. Netting to prevent bird damage is essential.

### Picking

Remove the ripe berries by pinching through the stalk half an inch from the fruit. This avoids any bruising to the ripe fruit.

## Strawberry runners

This is a way of propagating new plants. The runners develop not long after the fruit starts to form. If you require some more plants, peg down the runners into the soil. They should root quickly and can be removed and planted in early autumn, but only propagate from clean and healthy stock. If you do not require the runners for propagation, cut them off as they will take energy from the crop.

## Best varieties

**Florence:** A new introduction with a wonderful flavour and excellent disease resistance.

**Hapil:** Season mid-June to mid-July. Very popular variety – good in dry summers. Very high yield and well-shaped glossy fruit.

**Honeoye:** One of the earliest varieties. Fine flavour and bright shiny fruits.

**Rhapsody:** Good late variety. Good resistance to Powdery Mildew, Red Cored and Wilt.

**Symphony:** Very vigorous plants. Strong grower and heavy cropper.

**Perfection:** Has unusual pink flowers.

**Eros:** This variety does well in Yorkshire. Excellent, good flavoured and enjoys cool conditions.

Perfection strawberries are distinguished by their unusual pink flowers.

# Blackcurrants

## Soil condition

Blackcurrants enjoy heavy rather than sandy light soil, yet it should be well drained with one good barrowful of well-rotted farmyard manure dug in for each plant. Prepare planting stations well in advance to allow soil to settle down and compact. Blackcurrants like firm soil.

## Propagation

Propagate only from healthy plants. October is a good time. Choose well-ripened shoots of the current season's growth twelve to fourteen inches long. It is not essential to cut below a node, as they will root readily wherever the cuts are made. Take out a slit trench six inches deep and firm in well. The buds quickly form shoots, which lead to the formation of the bush. With blackcurrants we are constantly looking for strong shoots from the base.

Leave the cuttings in situ until the following October and then plant in their permanent position. You can either leave them 3ft 6in apart and unpruned to fruit a little in its first season, or prune down to four inches to establish a strong bush.

Another way to produce a quick crop is to put cuttings six inches apart in an area a yard square and allow them to fruit in their first year. When the berries are ripe, cut off the shoot three inches from ground level and bring indoors to pick. The cuttings will grow well in situ the following year.

## Pruning

You can prune established blackcurrant bushes as soon as the crop has been harvested by taking out one third of the older branches. This induces new growth from the base and maintains the vigour. Retain strong young base shoots evenly spaced round the bush.

## Feeding

Blackcurrants enjoy nitrogen so give a dressing of poultry manure evenly as a mulch in April. In the autumn apply three ounces of sulphate of potash to each bush and hoe in gently to avoid root disturbance. Water well in dry weather as the berries are swelling.

My father grew fantastic fruit bushes. He used to water with liquid sheep manure, and he was also good with the shotgun. Dad used to clean and gut rabbits, dig holes near to the bushes and bury the cleanings – and had blackcurrants as big as grapes!

## Varieties

**Ben Sarek:** Season mid-July. Good for small gardens. Short compact bushes and large fruit.

**Ben Lomond:** Late July and August. Very sweet, good resistance to mildew, heavy cropper.

**Malling Jet:** Late August. Large crop of huge berries – up to twenty per sprig.

**Boskop:** Early July. Ripens quickly, very high vitamin C content.

# Redcurrants and Whitecurrants

Blackcurrants will tolerate a bit of shade. Redcurrants and whitecurrants like to be grown in an open sunny position.

## Soil conditions

Well-drained site, medium loam with plenty of moisture-retentive material added. Well-rotted farmyard manure is ideal to dig in prior to planting. Established bushes require one ounce per square yard of sulphate of ammonia in the spring and one ounce of sulphate of potash in the autumn.

## Propagation

From clean and healthy stock that is well ripened take year-old growths twelve to fourteen long. Remove the lower buds from the cuttings. This gives a clean area of stem called a leg. Red and white currants are best grown in this way with no shoots coming from below the soil. When inserting the cuttings make a slit trench four inches deep. Place cuttings into the trench and firm in well. Leave in the cutting trench for a year. They can then be planted into permanent quarters a yard apart.

## Pruning

Winter pruning on established bushes is done by cutting back all leading shoots by a third. Shorten all side growths to four buds.

July pruning helps to promote fruit bud formation. Shorten the side growths to six leaves but leave the leading shoots unpruned at this time.

Another good way to grow red and white currants is a double cordon. They can then be grown against a wall, planting distance two feet apart. This way you get extra large fruit.

## Protection

When redcurrants start to ripen, birds are very attracted so at this stage make sure they are netted.

## Varieties – Redcurrant

**Red Lake:** Very high quality fruit, scarlet and very juicy.

**Roxby Red:** Season late July. Outstanding quality and good flavour.

**Laxtons Number One:** Excellent flavour. Firm berries – not as large as Red Lake but ripens earlier.

## Whitecurrant

**White Grape:** Excellent flavour huge berries even in Yorkshire makes wonderful jelly and wine.

# Gooseberries

This is a fruit that does well in cooler areas – and thus in Yorkshire. A good fruit bush for smaller gardens, it can easily be trained as a double or triple cordon. This method is ideal for growing on walls or fences.

## Location

With gooseberries flowering in the early part of the year, they should not be planted in low-lying frosty areas. A position in full sun would be ideal.

## Propagation

Gooseberries are propagated in October by hardwood cuttings nine to twelve inches long. As with red and white currants, they should be grown on a leg. This means that when making the cutting you remove the lower buds, which should give a six-inch bare stem without suckers.

## Soil conditions

Gooseberries will tolerate most soil, although it should be well drained. If you have a light sandy soil, dig in well-rotted manure to survive the moisture. If your soil is very heavy, try and improve by digging in well-rotted straw.

## Planting

Best carried out from November to February with a planting distance four feet apart. Plant firmly and mulch around the plants in spring with rotted compost. Apply two ounces of sulphate of potash around each plant to avoid early defoliation. Wood ash scattered around the bushes is also a good organic form of potash. Too much nitrogen gives soft growth and can induce American gooseberry mildew.

## Pruning

Summer pruning should be in July. Cut back side shoots to six leaves, which helps to improve blossom bud formation.

The main pruning season is winter. If you are troubled with birds eating buds, it may be as well to leave until February. Shorten back leading growths by one-third and prune all side shoots to one and a half inches. If extra large berries are required on dessert types, prune side shoots to two buds to make open-centred bushes. Upright growing bushes should be pruned to outward-facing buds and weeping bushes to upward-facing buds.

### Hinnonmaki Red

Season late July. Very good resistance to American gooseberry mildew. Fruit is sweet and aromatic.

### Hinnomaki Yellow

Like the red variety, good resistance to American gooseberry mildew. Fruit slightly smaller with a superb flavour.

### Keepsake

Early July. The plant has a spreading habit and is a prolific cropper.

### Hero of the Nile

Pale green to white fruits, exceptionally large. The growth arches.

### Guido

Early July. Large red and hairy fruits.

### Invicta

Late July – dessert and culinary use. Fruit very large, skin pale green and slightly hairy. Very good resistance to American gooseberry mildew.

### Pax

Season mid-July. Dessert type, good resistance to American gooseberry mildew, almost thornless.

### Woodpecker

Holds the record for the heaviest gooseberry. Huge size, good flavour.

# Raspberries

Raspberries tend to be less productive than many crops, often due to virus diseases. It is of the utmost importance to start off with first-class stock certificates issued by DEFRA. Healthy vigorous stock should give you good crops for five or six years. Always buy from reputable stockists.

## Soil conditions, preparation and weed control

It is very important to start off with a weed-free site. Raspberry plants are very shallow rooting and great damage to root systems can easily happen. If you are continuously weeding or if you get bindweed, this can quickly choke out the plants. With raspberries we are constantly looking out for young growth emerging from the root system to give new fruiting canes each year. If the soil is matted with weeds, the young growths are inhibited and can break off when weeding.

Good ground preparation for raspberries can take almost a year. They do not like lime, which can induce yellowing of the leaves and result in a poor crop. Apply one barrowful of well-rotted compost or farmyard manure to each square yard. When digging, remove all perennial weeds. With raspberry roots being very shallow and young growth emerging all the time from the base, it is a good ploy to apply phosphate. It will guard against a shortage and get a good vigorous root system established.

Apply a mulch of manure after planting and in each successive year. Stable manure with plenty of straw is ideal – one barrowful to a two yard run of row. A spring dressing each year should comprise half an ounce of sulphate of potash and one ounce of sulphate of ammonia to the yard run of row. An excess of nitrogen will increase cane growth but will not give higher yields. Yet a deficiency of potash will definitely give lower yields.

## Planting

Can be done any mild period from the end of October till early March, sooner rather than later. Avoid planting when the soil is too wet and during frosty weather. Make sure the roots are wet. You may need to soak them in a bucketful of water, as the roots can often be very dry in transit from the supplier. Sometimes they are even packaged in dry peat.

Raspberry canes need shallow planting. My method on a well-prepared area of clean soil is to take out a shallow trench of say a spade's width. Each plant is then held vertically. Spread the root out, backfill and firm well in with the sole of your foot. Do not plant deeply. This can often be gauged by the soil mark on the base of the plants. A general guideline is to cover roots with three inches of soil.

## Pruning and growing

What a bonus! On the 5th of November not only do we get an explosion of fireworks but we are in the midst of an explosion of flavour. It is the joy of autumn raspberries.

My six plants of All Gold were planted in December in a Link-a-Bord raised bed. The soil had been improved by digging in a barrowful of well-rotted farm manure. The plants were spaced two feet apart. To each station I added a large handful of sheep manure pellets, which as stated in other chapters are slow release and full of wool fibres. They rot down over a long period and create plant food organically.

The treatment of autumn-fruiting raspberries is very different to their summer relatives. With summer fruiters you cut out the old stems after fruiting in say August or September. With the autumn types, all growths are cut back to ground level in February. At this stage I apply a two-ounce dressing of sulphate of potash around each plant and watch them grow. By August they are six feet tall and need supporting. I attach the canes to string, which is fastened to plastic-coated wires fixed to poles eight feet apart.

Look forward to the thrill of fresh raspberries from your own garden!

## Summer Fruiting Varieties

**Glen Ample:**  Season late July. Big yields of sweet fruits with good colour and shape. Spine free, which makes picking easy.

**Glen Cova:**  Early July – one of the first to be picked. Small fruit but plentiful.

**Glen Magna:**  Mid-July to mid-August. Excellent flavoured large berry, almost spine-free canes.

**Glen Moy:**  Mid-June – I think this is the earliest of all the varieties. Tasty medium-size berries.

**Tulmaneen:**  Late July to late August. Now one of the most popular varieties in the UK with a long picking season.

The orange-yellow fruits of All Gold have a distinct look and taste. They are my favourite raspberries.

## Autumn Fruiting Varieties

Fruit in the autumn right up to the first hard frost.

**All Gold:**  Orange-yellow fruiting with a distinct sweet flavour – my favourite.

**Polka:**  Earliest of all the autumn-fruiting varieties, plugging the gap between the summer and autumn.

*Part 2. Fruit and Herbs*

# Blueberries

In recent years Blueberries have become a very popular fruit to be grown in the garden. I think it is because the berries are now very expensive.

## Soil conditions

Blueberries are a close relative of the bilberry and enjoy acid soil. They will not tolerate any lime, so they need conditions similar to moorland soil. Many people believe that blueberries are best grown in ericaceous compost. So if the soil in your garden is not on the acid side, you will have to grow them in containers filled with either leaf mould mixed with peat and acid soil or buy ericaceous compost. The ideal container is half a wooden barrel. They really seem to enjoy being grown in something so big, but make sure there are drainage holes in the base.

Blueberries are a well worthwhile garden plant as they are doing something all the year round. During the winter their highly coloured stems are almost as good as the attractive dogwood or cornus. In early spring the plump flower buds are very attractive. The flowers are extremely graceful and are followed by green berries, which ripen from June onwards depending on the variety. When the berry has ripened the colour varies from sky blue and purple to almost black. The berries then need protecting from the birds.

In the autumn, blueberrries give you superb colour with leaves a vibrant red to orange.

## Pruning

In the early years little or no pruning is required, apart from some of the very strong growths that can attain a height of five feet. In this case it is necessary to pinch out the growing tip, which will make the lateral growths develop that will eventually produce abundant fruit.

## Varieties

**Blue Crop:** Season July and August. Maybe the most popular variety. The light blue can crop up to 12lb per bush.

**Blue Ray:** July and August – huge fruit. Likes to be grown in a warm and sunny position, giving bright red stems and wonderful autumn foliage

**Darrow:** Huge fruit cropping in August. Introduced in 1965.

**Spartan:** Early July and August. Very vigorous upright plant. Can attain the height of five feet.

**Elliot:** July, August and into September. Good late variety.

# Loganberries and Blackberries

The loganberry is very productive and the fruit has a pleasant flavour. Loganberries are much larger than raspberries and are borne on natural shoots growing off the vigorous canes. Owing to the length of these shoots, strong wire supports are required to hold the fruiting canes in place. The supporting wires should be eighteen inches apart with the highest six feet off the ground. Loganberry plants should be grown eight feet apart and the canes trained fanwise onto the supporting wires. Plants must be kept in bounds by limiting the number of canes to the plant.

Fruit appears in the second season on lateral shoots that also bear flowers. At the same time new canes will grow from the plant base. These should be trained in and the old fruiting canes cut back. Place a mulch of old manure around the base of the plant during the summer time to retain the moisture. Loganberries like plenty of sun and a sheltered position.

Varieties include Loganberry Thornless and Loganberry Bauer.

Summer fruit at its finest. Clockwise
from top: Blackcurrants (Ben Sarek);
raspberries (Ben Magna); raspberries
(All Gold); redcurrants (Roxby red);
strawberries (Eros); gooseberries (Pax).

## Questions and Answers

*1. What is the best way to stop the birds eating all our soft fruit?*
Either use nets over the bushes or build a fruit cage with small mesh so that the birds cannot enter.

*2. Our strawberries are getting smaller than they have been for ten years. Is this normal?*
Strawberry plants should be removed after four years.

*3. Which are the best-flavoured strawberries?*
I like the varieties Symphony and Eros – they make my mouth water! Pick them on a warm summer's day.

Blackberries require similar conditions and treatment to loganberries but do better on a heavier soil.

## Varieties

**Bedford Giant:** Ready in late August or September. Very vigorous.

**Himalayan Giant:** Early September. Vigorous and very thorny. Each plant can provide 25lb of fruit.

**John Innes:** September and October. Heavy crop of extremely large fruit with a good flavour. Almost spineless.

This should keep them out! A
home-made bird-proof cage.

*Part 2. Fruit and Herbs*

Temptation strawberries soon
become very tempting!

# Rhubarb

You either love it or hate it, but to me rhubarb pulled fresh from the garden is a superb eating experience. I gather it, cut off the leaves and cube it into two-inch lumps. I then put it in a pan with loads of sugar, very little water and in ten minutes it's done. From March until the soft fruit starts in June, I have rhubarb three times a week with loads of cream and plenty of sugar. I am six-foot tall and weigh under eleven stones, so I need plenty of cream and sugar with my delicious rhubarb. Add cold or hot custard or cream and it is wonderful.

**4. There is a strawberry variety called Temptation that is grown from seed. How long before it fruits?**
The photograph was taken five months after sowing. I was already looking forward to being tempted by Temptation.

**5. When do we clean up the strawberry bed?**
October is a good time to remove any unwanted runners as well as brown and damaged leaves.

**6. When do we prune blackcurrants?**
Best done in November, removing one third of the old wood after four years.

**7. Our gooseberries always lose their leaves in May. Why?**
This is due to an attack of gooseberry sawfly, which is a tiny caterpillar. Spray with a systemic insecticide as soon as the plant comes into leaf.

**8. When do we plant raspberry canes?**
Normally in October and March, but container-grown plants can be planted at any time of year.

**9. Will blueberries do well where bracken has been growing?**
In general terms, bracken or fern grow on very acid soil. This is what blueberries like.

Rhubarb fresh from the garden
– a superb eating experience.

## Ground preparation

Dig in plenty of farmyard manure. The rhubarb farmers use shoddy from the wool industry, which has a slow release effect, to feed the roots over a long period. Rhubarb loves to be grown on rich land.

## Planting

November till March, bare rooted, with the crown bud level with the soil.

## Aftercare

The worst problem with the rhubarb crop is weeds. It is very difficult to spray for weed control so the land should be as weed-free as possible before planting. Water well in dry weather conditions.

## Pulling

Allow new Rhubarb plants to grow away strongly before you start to pull. They can be into full cropping after three years and will go on in same area for nine years. When harvesting rhubarb, slide a finger down the flange or socket. Take great care not to damage the growing bud and then pull away from the plant.

## Dividing

This is done when crowns are over five years old. When rhubarb starts to grow seed heads it tells you it is ready for splitting and moving. Split down to a single crown bud – and take care not to damage it. I use an old wood saw to cut through the chunky root.

## Growing on

I give a mulch of old rotted straw manure in spring before growth begins. This helps to retain moisture and keep weeds down.

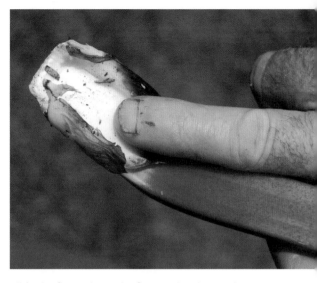

Slide the finger down the flange when harvesting rhubarb.

Seed heads on rhubarb are a sign that it is time to divide the plant.

*Part 2. Fruit and Herbs*

# Questions and Answers

**1. Can rhubarb be grown from seed?**
Yes – it is best sown in March time.

**2. Why does rhubarb go to flower?**
When rhubarb has been planted in the ground for many years it has a tendency to go to seed. This tells the gardener it is time to split the plant down to individual crowns and replant.

**3. How do you force rhubarb?**
Rhubarb is forced by eliminating all light. This is easily done in the garden by the use of an old dustbin. In January cover the crown with straw and put the dustbin over it. By mid-February you should be pulling rhubarb from your garden.

**4. What are the best varieties of rhubarb?**
Timperley Early is very good for early use. Victoria and Cawood Delight are also excellent varieties.

**5. What is a rhubarb crown?**
This is the root with the crown bud, out of which grow the sticks of rhubarb. Crowns need to be at least 2ft 6 in apart.

**6. Where is the rhubarb triangle?**
Yorkshire is well known for its rhubarb and the triangle is the area that embraces
Wakefield, Rothwell, Pudsey and Leeds.

**7. Do we have to feed and water rhubarb once it has been planted?**
Rhubarb is a gross feeder. I think mulching around the plants with old manure is a good idea and plenty of water in dry weather is essential.

**8. I have been told rhubarb leaves are poisonous. Can we put them on the compost heap?**
A small layer of leaves does not cause a problem, although it is said that they are toxic.

**9. Can rhubarb be grown in pots?**
I would suggest that something as big as a dustbin with holes in the base would be okay.

Rhubarb seed.

A rhubarb plant two months after sowing.

Rhubarb that has gone to flower.

Cawood Delight – an excellent variety of rhubarb.

A herb garden close to the house is a huge bonus.

# The Herb Garden

These days herbs are very popular and most of them easy to grow yet quite expensive to buy. Every modern house has racks or shelves of dry herbs.

Do try and grow your own in the garden. Make a plot near the house, where you can even pick herbs in the dark with a torch. What a bonus to nip out of the house, gather a few leaves of fresh herbs and cook or garnish with them within minutes of picking. The best place for a herb garden is a sloping site facing south or west, with a wall or fence at the back for a bit of protection. For ease of access, paving flags can be laid and individual square beds made from the slabs or flagstones.

When growing mints, which are very invasive, it may be necessary to curb the running roots by enclosing the area with some type of membrane or growing them in pots.

Very tall herbs like angelica should be placed at the back of the border and staked to avoid falling onto weaker subjects.

## Ground preparation

Dig deeply incorporating well-rotted farmyard manure and some bone meal. Most herbs thrive well on neutral soil pH7. If your soil is heavy and wet, drainage should be improved by adding grit.

Perennial herbs respond well to a dressing of moist peat or compost in early summer. This is best done after tidying up of the old dead growth, some of which requires cutting back in the autumn to avoid rotting the rest of the foliage in winter.

In general terms do not over-water because soft growth lacks flavour. Over-feeding should be avoided. Good compact plants routinely picked and pruned will maintain sufficient leaves for the household. Each year in the herb garden watch out for chance seedlings of annuals and biennials as these can perpetuate themselves very easily.

*Part 2. Fruit and Herbs*

Mint can readily be grown in pots, which will curb the running roots. Here are spearmint, variegated apple mint and white variegated mint.

Angelica – a very tall herb that should be placed at the back of the border.

When certain of the perennial herbs get too big, coarse or unruly, take off rooted pieces and replant. You can root many herbs by cuttings, layering or from seed.

When space is limited, lay out a gravel area and grow in pots or containers set on the gravel. This can look very attractive and is easy to maintain. Some of the more tender herbs like rosemary can easily be brought into the cold greenhouse for winter protection when grown in pots.

### Horseradish

A perennial herb with a thick rootstock and cylindrical fleshy roots. The leaves are large and dark green. It will grow well in most soils and is often seen on waste ground. Propagation by root cuttings is very easy. I just break off some strong thick chunks of root about three inches long and stick them upright in pots of soil. New plants appear in no time.

Horseradish is often served as a sauce or condiment to accompany cold meats. Its name means strong radish, with a hot burning sensation.

### Parsley

One of the most popular of our garden herbs. It is a biennial plant – you sow it one year and it will flower the next. In the meantime you can gather fresh sprigs. Parsley can be left to go to seed. Normally the soil can be hard and dry under the plant. Sometimes I fork through lightly giving a good watering around it. I then put

The Moss Curled variety of parsley.

Garden angelica in flower during its second year.

down some 'growbag' material just under the plant. When parsley is in full flower I insert a cane, which supports the seedhead and prevents the stem breaking off. When the flowerhead is very dry, the seed is then viable. I just shake the flowerhead and it drops onto the growbag material. Rake in the seed with your fingers. You will have a lot of parsley seedlings in about three weeks.

## Dill

An easily-grown annual herb. I normally sow a few seeds in small pots. When established, plant it in the herb garden. It is very useful in fish dishes and has a lovely aniseed flavour.

## Garlic

I have put garlic in my vegetable section, as it needs treating differently to other herbs.

## Sage

A perennial sub-shrub, it has a long taproot making the established plant difficult to move. It can be bought from nursery and garden centres as pot-grown plants. Can be grown from seed sown in springtime. Easily propagated from a heal cutting inserted into sandy and peaty compost, it likes well-drained, moisture-retentive soil.

One of the main uses for sage is flavouring in stuffing for poultry and pork. Sales of sage peak in the UK at Christmas time for turkey stuffing.

## Sweet marjoram

Often called pot marjoram, it can be grown from seed, rooted bits, or by dividing up the plants and replanting. Grows well in most soil types but likes to be well drained and enjoys lime. Sweet marjoram is great for flavouring soups, sauces and meat dishes. It is also said to aid digestion and has properties to alleviate rheumatism.

Sweet marjoram is an annual, unlike wild marjoram, which is a biennial.

## Garden angelica

A big and robust biennial herb that makes a short joined plant in its first season. In its second year it becomes a vast plant with a large flowerhead. Tends to self-seed with seedlings appearing everywhere. Used in confectionery as candy sweets.

*Part 2. Fruit and Herbs*

## Tarragon

A perennial herb with a rhizome root that makes propagation easy. Divide and replant or take cuttings with a heal of the old wood in springtime. Will thrive in most well-drained soils. No garden should be without tarragon as a few leaves will flavour salads, stew, sauces and pickles. Tarragon vinegar can be made before the plant flowers by steeping fresh leaves in a good white wine vinegar. Leave for about three weeks, strain and keep in small bottles for use.

## Thyme

Garden thyme, a native of the Mediterranean, is a perennial dwarf sub-shrub that is easy to propagate from cuttings. Likes very well drained moisture-retentive land. Grows very well in troughs and pots. Often used in flower gardens where a dwarf subject needs to hug the ground, as in floral clocks and bedding schemes. The variegated form is useful for planting in dry crazy-paving cracks. The perfume and fragrance gives off a nice smell when you walk through it.

Thyme is very much the essential ingredient in Bouquet Garnie, but use with care in stews, soups and meat dishes as it has a very strong flavour. In the spirit industry it is used to give flavour and aroma to Benedictine.

## Rosemary

An evergreen sub-shrub that flowers in April and May. It is often planted in the flower garden. One of the best varieties is Mrs Jessop. Rosemary does well in large pots and is very easily grown from seed and from cuttings taken from non-flowering shoots. Excellent to accompany lamb and wonderful for seasoning.

## Chives

Very useful clump-forming herb with attractive purple-blue flowerheads. Easy to propagate from seed or divide up an established plant. Likes fertile well-drained soil. It also makes a useful subject for growing in pots.

Excellent for use in salads and as chopped chives in cream cheese sandwiches with a few potato crisps. I could eat one now with a glass of light ale! Chives have a quite strong onion flavour, so eat a few mint leaves to make your breath smell nice.

Thymes look well where a dwarf subject needs to hug the ground.

A purple-blue flower is an attractive feature of chives.

# Questions and Answers

### 1. How do I dry herbs?

Herbs can be dried quite easily by laying in wooden slatted boxes or trays that can be stacked on top of each other. Ideal are trays for tomatoes, which have a wooden block in each corner to make stacking easy. They can be stood on the floor, which will readily dry the herbs. Check regularly and turn the herbs daily to ensure a proper access of air. An ideal place is a dry shed or greenhouse. Herbs can also be tied in bunches and strung up to dry, stems upwards, in flowing air. The bunches should be small enough so that they can dry easily all the way through. Another way to dry herbs is on a rack above a boiler in open paper bags.

### 2. How do I freeze herbs?

Herbs can be frozen either in aluminium foil, cut up in water in ice trays or in plastic bags.

### 3. Can herbs like chives, parsley and dill bought at supermarkets be grown in the garden?

It is very difficult to establish herbs bought in this way because they are often produced multi-sown in pots, grown in high temperatures and often out of season.

### 4. Can herbs be grown in hanging baskets?

Certain herbs can be grown in hanging baskets. I have been very successful with parsley because a hanging basket near the house is very convenient.

### 5. What are the best herbs for pots?

Rosemary, chives, parsley, sage and especially mint. This curbs the root run of mint and stops it invading the garden.

### 6. I have a fluted herb pot that is quite small. What can I grow in it?

Thymes are particularly suited to growing in small areas and will survive drought much longer than other subjects .

### 7. Are nasturtiums classed as herbs because we eat the flowers and leaves in salads?

Nasturtiums feature in every herb book – and also in every seed catalogue. There is a wonderful perennial form, which is a double called Hermine Grassaph. So I am also a bit confused. Let's say it is a tongue-in-cheek herb – an annual and perennial.

### 8. My rosemary always gets burnt by the frost in the spring. Is there a solution?

The best solution is to grow rosemary in a container so it can be brought into a cool greenhouse for its protection in bad weather.

### 9. Each year my parsley goes to seed. Can I save my own seed?

Parsley seed is easy to save. As it is a biennial it will always go to seed in its second year. Wait until the seedhead is dry and then fasten a brown paper bag over it. When ripe the seed will fall into the bag. Put it in packets, keep in a drawer, and label.

### 10. How do I grow flat-leaf parsley?

Use the variety Italian Plain. I sow the seed in trays in a warm greenhouse in February, and prick out individual seedlings into small pots for planting out in May. We can pick leaves most of the year if there is a mild winter. The plant comes back strongly until April time. By then it has finished its biennial cycle and goes to seed. Your own seed can be saved in exactly the same way as the curly parsley.

Hanging baskets that have developed in the greenhouse are by late May ready to hang outside.

# PART 3. FLORAL GLORY

As explained in the Introduction, this book deliberately avoids approaching subjects in a conventional order. Starting the pivotal section on Floral Glory with hanging baskets might seem a bit strange, but it recognises that many Yorkshire folk have virtually no garden at all. Hanging baskets are thus immensely popular in the county, as you can have wonderful displays of plants irrespective of ground area. It is not surprising that they have become one of the most popular of all aspects of modern-day horticulture.

I normally begin work on hanging baskets in early April, but the true herald of spring is undoubtedly snowdrops. It therefore seems only right that they should start the next section of this book on bulbs, which is followed by another of my all-time favourites – Sweet Peas. We then move on to bedding plants - both spring and summer – and a selection of herbaceous perennials.

# Hanging Baskets

One of the most popular places to site hanging baskets is near the front door of the house. What a welcome for the postman, the paper lad and the milkman!

I have got a tremendous excuse in summertime, as I make up the hanging baskets for my local pub. Betty will say to me in the evening, "Where are you going?"

"I am going to the Hunters Inn to feed the baskets." I reply.

"A likely story!" she says.

Many factors have to be considered when planting up hanging baskets. For example, the smaller the basket the more water it may need. If you are out at work all day in the summertime, a small basket full of plants will dry out very quickly to the extent it may never recover.

The different types of hanging baskets range from wire to wickerwork. They include plastic baskets with ready-made holes into which you can pop the plants. There are also very traditional wall baskets based on feeding hayracks, or mangers, which in the past were used to hold the hay for farm animals. Some of these old-fashioned mangers are many years old, extremely sought-after and can bring large sums of money at farm auctions. Some of the hayracks are very large and look absolutely magnificent when planted up with trailing plants. When fastened securely to a stark wall of a house, the striking effect of magnificent colour can bring a new dimension to the outside appearance of any property. The combination of fixed wall baskets and hanging baskets either side of the house door can be

Hayrack basket ten days after planting. When a basket is a permanent feature on a house wall, it may be necessary to plant directly into it. I usually wait until June, so that hopefully the frosts have gone and the weather is improving.

stunning.

My favourites are eighteen to twenty-inch wire baskets with connecting chains and a ring at the top to hang on a hook above the door. A twenty-inch basket should be deep enough to take twenty litres of compost. This is enough to enable plants to survive during the summer period providing you have the facility to give plenty of water.

## Preparation

What type of liner do we use in the basket? Some people use plastic dustbin liners, while others prefer sphagnum moss or coconut fibres. I use a product made from sheep's wool called Woolmoss, which I find absolutely superb. It looks a lot better than a bin liner and it is also moisture retentive, which is very important in helping to look after the baskets in hot weather. I start off by covering the base of the basket with Wooolmoss and then going up the sides for a couple of inches.

## Compost

I always put in some bulky material, such as bits of rotted turf or old manure, into the base of the basket. This acts as a reservoir to retain moisture and gives the roots something to which they can attach. I use a very good quality multipurpose compost with added sheep manure pellets. One small handful to a twenty-inch basket will keep the plants well fed during the summer months.

## Planting up

I start to plant up my hanging baskets in early April. At this time of the year the plants are quite small, which makes it easy to work them into the sides of the baskets as the root ball area is just getting established. With it being early season, it is very important when making up the baskets that they are hung inside a cold greenhouse. This helps the young plants grow on well, as many of them are tender and very susceptible to the cold weather conditions.

I like to start with the long trailing plants. These hang down like a long skirt and give the basket stature and great depth. So in the second week in April I put in my first layer and then leave it to get established. After ten days I plant the second layer of petunias,

Young plants in baskets developing in the greenhouse in mid-May.

marigolds, violas and the like. I let these get established, and then moss up the rest of the basket and add more compost. Finally I complete the basket by planting the rim and the rest of the top. The plants for the rim are grown on in modules in small pots and can include ivy leaf, geraniums, trailing fuchsias, begonias and busy lizzies. These then grow and slip over the edges of the basket.

## Aftercare

Hanging baskets only have space for a small amount of compost, as the root development is quite vast. The roots soon get starved of food and water. When well established, it is essential at all times that the baskets are kept moist and fed with liquid fertiliser. Feed normally every ten days and make sure the compost is moist in order to avoid root burn.

Constantly pick over the baskets removing dead flowerheads, damaged leaves and seedpods.

## Joe's Tip

When hanging up the basket after planting I always get some thin strong wire. This is used to help strengthen the chains. I connect the wire to the rim of the basket, and thread it through the chain and up to the top ring. This strengthening wire will stop the basket from falling on to the postman's head!

## Plant material

The following is a list of plant types and varieties that I use successfully in baskets and hayracks:

**Begonias Illumination:** All colours, trailing types.

**Begonias Nonstop:** All colours, good for planting around top rim.

**Begonias Semperflorens:** Mixed, good for side planting in hayracks and baskets. Cocktail series is an excellent choice.

**Bidens:** Wonderful plant that gives a long yellow trail.

**Brachycome:** Often called Swan river daisy. Produces a multitude of single daisy-shaped flowers in all shades of blue – a must for every basket.

**Cineraria maritima:** Silver Dust variety makes a wonderful centre point in baskets.

**Geraniums:** All types are good for planting at the top of the basket and will flower all summer long.

**Ivy-leafed geraniums:** Make a wonderful cascading habit in the sides or round the rim of the basket.

**Impatiens (Busy Lizzies):** The most colourful of all basket plants. No hanging basket should be complete without it! I like the F1 Super Elfin series, which has a mixture of pink, white, red, lavender and violet colours.

**Lobelias:** The trailing forms are another must for baskets. I like the Fountain Mixed variety with shades of pink, blue and white. The String of Pearls variety is also a delightful cascading mixture.

**Mimulus:** Very early flowering. Gives the basket a good start for the flowering season.

**Nasturtiums:** Provide a great cascading effect, although they sometimes get too vigorous. The Alaska series with its marbled foliage is very striking. I have seen nasturtiums touch a doorstep six feet beneath the basket. Some people have problems with blackfly and caterpillars.

**Pansies and Violas:** Another subject well used in baskets. I particularly like the F2 hybrid Jolly Joker with the diffusion of orange and purple. Another F2 hybrid, Padparadja, is bright orange in colour and was named after a precious stone from Sri Lanka.

Hanging baskets should be kept moist and fed often to remain in tip-top condition.

**Petunias:** Another must for colour throughout the summertime – especially the cascading types.

**Sweet Peas:** The Cupid series have a dwarf pendula effect and add fantastic perfume to any basket.

I always use plants like nepta, which is variegated catmint, variegated ivies, verbena tapiens, scaevola and variegated ivies to give the wonderful skirt at the base of the basket.

## Central feature

Fuchsias make an eye-catching centrepiece and balance up the whole of the basket. If you want an architectural feature, the stunning formation of leaves from a corderline is also very attractive.

*Part 3. Floral Glory*

# Questions and Answers

**1. Is it necessary to use moisture retentive gels in hanging baskets?**
Lots of people use polymer gels in the compost. It has the effect of increasing the capacity of the compost to hold moisture.

**2. I have a problem with snails climbing into the basket. What should I do?**
What a luxury to be sat with wonderful fresh leaves to eat all summer long in the moist conditions of a basket! I always suggest using slug control in hanging baskets, and be watchful as they can always be picked out when you see them.

**3. Can plug plants be planted directly into the basket?**
Yes – providing you have conditions for these young plants to grow. Certainly a greenhouse is necessary early in the year, but I prefer to grow the plants in small pots or modules before planting into the basket.

**4. Some people say water systems are necessary for hanging baskets. Is this correct?**
To have an automatic water system that comes on in the evening is a very useful addition. It makes the care of baskets and mangers much easier.

**5. What are the best fuchsia varieties to give the pendula effect in the baskets?**
La Campanella is extremely free flowering with a free branching habit. Cascade and Marinka are all wonderful trailing fuchsias.

**6. What is a good fuchsia for the central feature?**
Celia smedley is very free flowering and upright with large flowers. The Display variety is very upright, making a wonderful focal point.

**7. Is it possible to save my plants from one year to another?**
If you are lucky enugh to have a heated greenhouse, many of the subjects we have mentioned can be kept through the winter and propagated by cuttings for the following year. Plants like geraniums and fuchsias can be taken out and potted but will need frost protection during the winter months.

**8. Can my hanging basket be saved from one year to another?**
I once saved a hanging basket in a cold greenhouse and let it go completely dry. I covered it with garden fleece and it came through the winter with few losses.

Pouches that have been unhooked to give the plants a good soaking with a hosepipe.

**9. Is the variety Verbena peaches and cream suitable for a basket?**
Peaches and cream is a wonderful combination of pastel shades from apricot to orange. I have used it with great success in baskets.

**10. When I go on holiday I have nobody to look after my baskets. What is the best thing to do?**
Unhook your baskets off the wall and set them in a shady area for the duration of your holiday. Make sure they are well watered before you go away and check immediately on your return. However, there is no substitute for getting a friendly neighbour to pop in three times a week.

**11. I like to plant up flower pouches with Busy Lizzies, but I can never keep them wet enough. Have you any ideas?**
Yes – I unhook the pouches, lay them flat and give them a good soaking with the hosepipe.

# A Partridge not in a Pear Tree

The partridge and its chicks – and the nest that was definitely not in a pear tree!

O ne Monday morning in late May we set off to collect twelve large hayrack mangers. The purpose of the visit was to bring the mangers back to the nursery, so I could replant them for the summer season. It was a journey through splendid Yorkshire countryside with pheasants and partridges in the fields. We arrived at a beautiful house and garden attended by a lovely lady called Jill and started to unhook the hayrack mangers off the walls. We unhooked the last basket right next to the busy back door of the house. Walking back to the van, I suddenly noticed a movement in the basket. To my amazement there was a partridge sat on a nest. Partridges usually nest on the ground, certainly not six feet above it, and normally in a wood, next to a bank or behind a fallen tree. This one had also endured the discomfort of being watered twice a day with the automatic water system!

Our movement disturbed the bird, so she jumped off the nest and ran under my van. Just then Jill came out of her house and was told about the partridge. We decided to put the manger back in position. Very quickly the bird was back on the nest and sitting snugly on her eggs.

A few days later the housekeeper heard a commotion outside the door. It was the mother partridge calling out, and thirteen chicks then jumped and fell out of the nest. When all were present she marched them on to the front lawn of the house. She then sat up and all the chicks disappeared under her wings. So this partridge was certainly not in a pear tree!

# Snowdrops

A large clump of Sam Arnott snowdrops.

When snowdrops have been grown closely together they multiply very well by forming many new bulbs each year. Eventually it gets to a point when the vigour can be reduced, and sometimes dying out can happen. A new lease of life for the plants can be achieved when the clumps are split up and divided and replanted. The divided clumps should contain about fifteen to twenty growing bulbs on the point of flower. Good results can be obtained by splitting when clumps are emerging through the ground, and replanting at this stage. Many people split and replant when going out of flower but still when green growth is present.

Soil conditions should be well drained yet moisture retentive. A good way to plant into grassed areas for naturalising the snowdrops is to remove an area of turf, take out some of the old soil and backfill with some good compost. Firm in well making sure the bulbs are covered by at least an inch of soil, and then replace the turf.

Snowdrops can be planted as small dry bulbs in the autumn but these take quite a while to get established. My method with such bulbs is to plant six in a three-inch pot and grow on in frames, then when they are just about to flower plant into the garden. This way they establish quickly.

## Varieties

**Galanthus elwesii:** A small narrow leaf form that flowers in early February.

**Galanthus nivalis 'Sam Arnott':** A wonderful variety. The outer petals are very short and broad. It can be seen growing very well in February in York Gate gardens in Leeds.

**Galanthus atkinsii:** Very narrow leaves. In my garden it is one of the last to flower. There is a heart-shaped green mark at the tip of each flower.

**Galanthus nivalis:** This is the one I call the wild snowdrop. It can be seen in its glory in orchards, churchyards and on grass verges. It has a wonderful scent, almost like honey. Very easily propagated by dividing the clumps.

**Galanthus Lady Beatrix Stanley:** A wonderful double form with a tiny green mark on the tip of each petal. Flowers in early March in my garden.

**Galanthus John Gray:** Has narrow grey green leaves with very large flowers, which appear in mid-February.

# The Feel Good Factor

I am going to make a very personal statement. My sap starts to rise when I first see snowdrops pushing through the garden soil. They are the true herald of spring. I think of them as being almost magical, growing through all the wet, cold, frost and snow. Then we get a little break in the weather and suddenly they are in flower – in very mild conditions we have had an occasional bloom at Christmas. It is normally late January through February and March.

I think that if snowdrops can perform their magic then I need to step up a gear. They tell me to get cracking so that I am off to a new gardening year with Galanthus nivallis – the true herald of spring. I just love the snowdrop. If I were stranded on a desert island and if I had a wish, my first three plants would be potatoes, sweet peas and Snowdrops.

We are lucky to live in a lovely Yorkshire village with lots of fantastic people. When I drove through one February day as the weather was improving, I saw many large clumps of snowdrops on the grass verges. I thought they needed splitting and replanting in areas when none were present and was sure that within three years we could see a magnificent carpet.

In conversation with my good friend, milkman and 'Lord Mayor' of Huby, Michael Styrin, we decided we will ask our friends to split up and transplant clumps of this wonderful plant all over our village. We will also ask them to divide those in their gardens, and give us their spare clumps so that we can plant on the verges of the main road. We want to give local people and car drivers the feel good factor and get rid of the winter blues.

In actual fact Michael is not a Lord Mayor. But we christened him this because of all the good he does, although sometimes he goes on a bit!

Do the same as we do – split and plant snowdrops everywhere.

Snowdrops are the true herald of spring and my sap starts to rise the moment they appear.

*Part 3. Floral Glory*

# Crocuses

I start whenever possible with crocuses in small pots. Use either John Innes No 1 or a good multipurpose compost. You can plant up to six crocus corms into a three-inch pot. By the first week in October the corms should be planted and placed in a cold frame until the point of flower, when they can then be moved into the garden.

Mice love to nibble the young succulent growths in early spring. If this is a problem trapping maybe the answer, or training a cat like my Fizz and allowing her to be on duty when the mice are about.

## Varieties
**Tommasinianus (Whitewell Purple):** Excellent variety of crocus that naturalises itself extremely quickly by producing many cormlets below ground. Also has great ability in producing young plants from seedpods.

**Golden Yellow Mammoth:** Amazing show when mass planted.

**Joan of Arc:** Very large white flowers.

**Rembrance:** Wonderful rich blue.

**Pickwick:** Silver with lilac stripes.

**Zwanenburg Bronze:** Golden yellow on bronze.

Whitewell Purple – an excellent variety of crocus.

# Hyacinths

Wonderful for forcing and excellent for bedding, hyacinths have got to be one of the most exotic of all perfumed plants.

## Varieties
**Delft Blue:** Dark blue with excellent perfume.
**Purple Sensation:** Wonderful purple colour.
**Pink Pearl:** Bright pink, very early.
**Jan Bos:** Very bright red.
**White Pearl:** Best of the whites.

# Daffodils and Narcissi

Daffodils and narcissi are split into many groups:

### Division 1a – Yellow Trumpets
**Golden Harvest:** Very old favourite, rich golden yellow.

**King Alfred:** Deeply frilled, still a firm favourite.

**Spellbinder:** Sulphur yellow trumpet turning to white.

### Division 1b – Bi-Coloured Trumpets
**Goblet:** Lemon and yellow trumpets

**Ellen:** New variety – pure white with giant pale yellow trumpets.

### Division 1c – White Trumpets
Mount Hood and Mrs R. Backhouse are the best varieties in this group.

### Division 2a – Large-Cupped Narcissi
Carlton and Fortune were respected varieties of yesteryear.

A wonderful display of Jet Fire narcissi.

## Division 2b – Small-Cupped Narcissi
**Flower Record:** Large white with pure orange centre.
**Ice Follies:** Creamy white opens to yellow.

## Division 4 – Narcissi
Golden Ducket: Fully double, broad petals, uniform pure yellow. I think this is the best variety in this group.

## Division 5 – Triandus Narcissi
Thalia: Two to three white flowers per stem, mid-April.

## Division 6 – Cyclamineus Narcissi
Fantastic group with my favourite Tête-à-Tête, February Gold and Jet Fire.

## Division 7 – Jonquilla Narcissi
Jonquilla Bellsong: Very scented.

## Division 8 – Tazetta Narcissi
These are the multi-headed fragrant varieties. Cheerfulness and Geranium are stunning.

## Division 9 – Poeticus Narcissi
Actea is the best in this group.

## Miniature Daffodils and Narcissi
Bulbocodium conspicuous, Canaliculaus and Little Gem all true miniature narcissi.

Another of my favourites in the same group is Tête-à-Tête.

When ordering daffodils and narcissi you will find that they are grouped into these different sections, which is more or less classed as the bible for all the different types .

When planting daffodil bulbs they are best grown on well-drained soil. The planting depth should be three times that of each bulb.

# Tulips

Like daffodils. tulips are split into different groups. In some of the groups there are hundreds of varieties. Tulips make wonderful displays in early spring – and they are fantastic for planting among spring-bedding plants like wallflower and polyanthus. Certain types are great in pots and containers, while others are wonderful for planting in rock gardens. Many varieties of tulips will naturalise themselves in your soil and will appear every spring for many years.

## Kaufmanniana

Exceptionally early on very short stems, these are often called the Water Lily tulip. Johann Strauss, Shakespeare and Fashion are all fantastic varieties.

## Gregii

Gregii are brilliant flowers and the leaves are marbled or striped. They are almost a permanent garden plant coming up year after year. Red Riding Hood, Pinocchio and Toronto often produce up to three flowers to a stem.

## Fosteriana

A hybrid race of tulip with brilliant oriental colours. Apricot Emperor, Orange Emperor and Rosy Dream are excellent varieties.

## Single Early Tulips

A group of tulips that are dwarf growing and excellent for bedding. They are one of the first to bloom outside. Brilliant star, Candy Prince and Charles are my favourites.

## Double Early Tulips

Flower at least three weeks behind Early Single Tulips. They have massive peony-shaped blooms and are very effective in beds and borders. Foxtrot, Evita and Double Prince give a magnificent show.

## Darwin

The largest and I think the most gorgeous tulip. Brilliant blooms on strong erect stems. Apeldoorn Beauty of Apeldoorn, Blushing Apeldoorn and Golden Apeldoorn make stunning displays in May.

## Triumph or Mid-Season Tulips

A cross between Darwin and Single Early Tulips, they have a strong habit with many brilliant colours. Bing Crosby, Blue Ribbon and Cheers are good types.

## Single Late or Cottage type

Possibly the latest flowering of the tulips, Queen of the Night is black in colour and is stunning.

## Lily Flowered

Possibly the tallest of all the tulips. White Triumphator, Red Shine and Ballerina are truly beautiful and can attain a height of almost three feet.

*

The range of bulbs is so vast that I have mentioned just the most popular types. Other bulbs include irises, scilla, winter aconites and muscari, which is the grape hyacinth.

# Questions and Answers

*1. What does it mean when referring to snowdrops planting in the green?*
Snowdrops can be dug out of the ground when they are growing and replanted back in again without any check to growth.

*2. How long can you leave bulbs growing in grass before you mow them off?*
Always leave at least six weeks for the foliage to die back and replenish the bulbs for the next year.

*3. What is the best way to get a nice bowl of hyacinths in full flower for Christmas Day?*
In late August and September, plant the bulbs in small pots with the tips just showing. Place them in a cold dark position and bring indoors three weeks before Christmas. When on the point of flower, transfer to a large bulb bowl. Use five or seven bulbs to the bowl. Father Christmas should be very pleased when he smells the gorgeous perfume on Christmas morning!

*4. How do you stop birds pecking crocus flowers?*
I place small canes among the crocus and tie black cotton to them. When the birds touch the cotton it frightens them.

*5. Is there an advantage in tying daffodils in a clump?*
I don't think there is any advantage. Let them die down naturally but remove all dead flowers and feed with liquid fertiliser after flowering.

*6. My daffodils have all gone blind. Why?*
This happens when they have been in the ground a long time. It indicates they want splitting up and replanting.

*7. Is there any advantage in putting bulbs in pots, growing on in frames and planting out at the point of flowering in spring?*
Yes – especially when the bulbs are small as with miniature daffodils and crocuses. It stops them being stolen by the squirrels. They establish themselves very quickly the following year.

*8.When bulbs have finished flowering is it best to dig them out of the ground and dry them?*
I prefer to leave the bulbs in the ground for six weeks to die down naturally. If you have to lift the bulbs it is best to heel them in. Lift them again later and dry them off.

*Part 3. Floral Glory*

# Sweet Peas

My summers would not be the same if I did not have Sweet peas growing. They take me back to my childhood when my father grew Sweet Peas in his garden and my mother constantly kept them in order by tying the plants to the canes almost every day. I will never forget the gorgeous perfume every time I walked past the plot where he grew about 500 plants of Sweet Peas.

Sweet Pea seedlings.

## Sowing Sweet Peas

For the earliest flowers autumn sowing is preferable, but early flowers can also be obtained from a January sowing. I have experimented with dates and between September 20 and October 12 is about right for autumn sowing. My method is to use a standard size seed tray and leave an inch gap between each seed.

I find the following mixture is ideal for Sweet Pea sowing and potting. I use four parts of good clean topsoil, one part sharp sand and one part of leaf mould or peat. No fertiliser is used at all at this stage. The soil needs to be moist as this can save the necessity of heavy top watering once sowing has taken place. Too much top water at sowing time can be detrimental to good germination. I believe elaborate composts are quite unnecessary and are often the cause of long, spindly and soft winter growth.

After sowing the boxes are placed into a cold frame and covered with newspaper. If it is hot and sunny this avoids excess drying out. Germination takes between ten and fourteen days. When it has occurred ventilation should be given and the glass frames can be removed in a few days. Replace the frames when frost is likely. During severe frost it may be advisable to cover the frames with mats. Keep them covered until the plants are thawed out should they become frozen.

## Potting on

When the seedlings have made their first true leaves, pot them into three-inch pots. Grow on in the cold frame using the same soil mixture as when they were sown. At this stage keep a watchful eye on slugs and mice as they can decimate the young plants.

## Care of plants during winter

Plants must be grown on very slowly and no attempt must be made to stimulate growth by feeding or keeping them warmer. Keep plenty of ventilation on the frames wherever possible. Nevertheless, pots or boxes should never be allowed to dry out. During heavy rainfall always try to get the frames back into position.

As soon as a Sweet Pea plant starts to grow, one shoot develops after about eight days and leaves begin to unfurl. When three sets of leaves have totally unfurled it is customary to remove the growing tip of the plant, as this stimulates the growth of side shoots from the base. It is necessary to grow these side shoots on during the winter months because the Sweet Pea plant rarely produces good blooms from the initial first growth. Autumn sown plants are usually ready for stopping in early November, and January sown plants can be stopped when they have made two pairs of leaves. The aim is to produce by March or April a short-jointed bushy plant which has been well hardened off.

## Ground preparation

It is no good at all raising perfect plants if the ground has not been adequately prepared to plant them. Preparation of the ground is best done during the Autumn so as to allow thorough consolidation during the winter. This ensures a firm root run, which is definitely conducive to short-jointed healthy growth during the growing season.

In the past, deep trenching was the way to prepare for the Sweet Peas. I feel that there is no need to go more than eighteen inches deep. Instead of opening up separate trenches it is best to double dig the area working in two-foot widths and make a thorough job of mixing both spits.

Over manuring, particularly with fresh manure should be avoided, and a medium dressing of old friable manure plus three ounces of bone meal to a square yard is quite adequate. Some old manure worked into the top spit and a dressing of wood ash will complete a totally sufficient preparation. During the week before planting, fork over the area to produce a fine tithe.

## Placing in the canes and support posts

To grow Sweet Peas well, it is a great advantage to have them on a single stem and to do this we have to place the canes in position prior to planting. I set my canes sixteen inches between the rows and twelve inches between the plants and I grow in double rows. It is an advantage to leave a four-foot space between the next row. It is necessary, before putting the canes into the soil, to knock in stout posts every four yards down each row. Attach a wire to the top of the posts running the full length of the row. This is necessary because the cane needs tying to the wire for support. When you put the canes into the soil, push them well in so that they are firm.

We are now ready for planting. Take out a planting hole with a trowel and knock the plant out of the pot. Some people say it is best to knock off the soil from the roots. All I do is to loosen the roots slightly at the base of the pots making sure that the roots are kept moist.

It is a great advantage to water the plants thoroughly the night before planting. Firm the plants in well. At this stage I would suggest you use slug

Seedlings ready for potting out.

Sweet Peas growing in a cold frame.

Short-jointed plants showing side shoot after stopping.

Removing tendrils from a Sweet Pea (see page 109).

Removing side shoots from established plants.

Strong supports for a single row of Sweet Peas. Twist the wire so that it grips tightly around the canes.

control as slugs are very partial to young Sweet Pea leaves. After planting, a light hoeing will finish the job off nicely and remove any solid areas.

## Tying in

When planting out, a good plant should have two strong side shoots. Ten days after planting I think it is a good idea to remove the weakest of shoots and tie in the strongest. This can be done using raffia, plastic-coated wire, Sweet Pea rings or twist ties. Some people have now gone upmarket and use a tying-in machine called the Max Tapener. This has got a plastic material and when you click the machine a wire staple holds everything together. It is an extremely quick method of tying. Sweet peas grow very quickly and it is necessary to tie at least three times a week.

## Cordon growing

I have already explained this method, which is just allowing one stem to be trained up one cane. It is the way the exhibitors grow their Sweet Peas. This ensures long flower stems, which are very straight with four flowers to each stem. To keep the plants strong it is necessary to remove the side shoots that grow in the leaf axels and also the tendrils. If these are left they tangle around the flowers.

## Feeding and watering

Watering is very important and it may be necessary to water at least once a week in dry weather conditions. This makes sure that the length of stem is maintained. When the Sweet Peas have reached the height of about six feet I give them a balanced liquid feed every fourteen days. It is necessary to keep cutting the flowers – the more you cut the more they produce.

## Pests of Sweet Peas

*The five enemies of the Sweet Pea grower are:*

**Slugs:** These are a pest especially during the winter. Under the pots in the cold frames is an ideal habitat for them; the best control is Slug Gone pellets.

**Mice:** Very fond of the Sweet Pea seed, they have also been known to nibble the young growths. Trapping is probably the best means of eradication.

**Birds:** Several birds – and especially the house sparrow – can devastate young plants and also be a menace by pecking the buds. I would suggest black cotton along the rows to help combat this problem or possibly using nets over the beds.

**Greenfly:** Possibly the worst enemy of the Sweet Pea; it undoubtedly carries the disease Mosaic. Greenfly can be very troublesome when the young plants are over wintering in the frames. Plants can be sprayed during the winter but avoid doing so during periods of frosty weather.

**Rabbits:** Known to eat plants up to two feet high. If this is a problem, the only way is to fence out the rabbits with wire mesh.

## Diseases and physiological disorders

Mosaic is the worst disease of Sweet Peas. It causes the growing point and its head to become distorted. It also causes mottling of the young leaves, which can be seen when held up to the light. The cause of this disease is a virus carried by greenfly. To combat it remove and burn any infected or suspected plants.

Cutting bushy pea sticks, with a good point on the stick for easy access.

## Growing Sweet Peas for ordinary garden culture

The method of cordon growing I have just explained is the way we produce top class blooms for exhibition work and cut flowers. However, some people may not have the time or inclination for the cordon system. Instead, they can obtain a wonderful and colourful display with some good quality blooms by allowing the plants to grow naturally in double rows or clumps. Instead of using canes, they can use bushy pea sticks six to eight feet high. Do not remove the tendrils as these cling to the sticks and help to support the plants. Thinning the number of growths to each plant will also improve the quality of the flowers. It is necessary to remove faded flowers otherwise they try to form seed pods to the detriment of healthy plant growth.

*Part 3. Floral Glory*

Betty Maiden, at the Chelsea Flower Show, with the variety of Sweet Pea named after her.

## Sweet Pea varieties

**Daily Mail:** A brand new variety. It has a bold, cerise pink colour with a creamy white base. It also has the advantage of often producing five blooms per stem.

**Betty Maiden:** Large heads of blue flake with a good strong stem and beautiful strong scent. Recommended by the RHS as an exhibition variety.

**Alan Williams:** Mid blue in colour, very good scent.

**Daphne:** Clear lavender with exhibition qualities, highly perfumed.

**Jane Amanda:** Rose pink on white

**Royal Wedding:** Excellent white medium scent.

**White Supreme:** One of the best whites, very highly scented.

**Beaujolais:** Deep burgundy maroon, very unusual colour.

**Joe Maiden:** New variety shortly to be introduced, with an unusual shade of red.

**Percy Thrower:** Lilac, very strong stems, highly scented.

**Mrs Bernard Jones:** Sugar pink.

My great friend Andrew Bean from Kippax is an excellent Sweet Pea breeder. Many years ago Andrew started trying to breed a yellow Sweet Pea and as a friend I would grow some seedlings each year, looking for the new colour. I planted some of Andrew's seedlings in April and in the row four plants developed very quickly. They were on the point of flower three weeks before the rest and I was excited when I saw the bud formation. They looked yellow but when they opened there were large heads of blue stripe with a dark lilac edge to each petal. When I first saw it, it was so different to anything else I had ever seen and the perfume was exotic. I eventually bought it from Andrew and started to reselect it back to one plant. It took four years to get the colour we wanted and it is now fixed and loved by many people.

I have only grown the variety Joe Maiden for two years. This is another seedling from Andrew and we hoped to fix it this year and try to explain the colour a little bit better than an 'unusual shade of red.'

'Joe Maiden' – a new variety of Sweet Pea in an unusual shade of red.

# Questions and Answers

### 1. Why do my Sweet Peas drop their buds?

Sweet peas often drop their buds during the early part of the growing season when the weather conditions fluctuate dramatically in temperature. They actually call it bud drop, which is a physiological disorder. It also happens when the Sweet Peas are growing away very quickly, but once it gets to the end of June it seldom occurs. It can be quite a problem in the early part of the year. Excessive feeding and overwatering can also affect the balance of growth, which sometimes results in bud dropping. I have noticed it is worse when we have a period of very hot days followed by very chilly nights.

### 2. What is a tendril?

A tendril is a series of tiny thin curling stems by which climbing plants cling to anything. If you are growing Sweet Peas by the cordon method it is necessary to remove the tendrils as these sometimes cling around the flowers and distort the petals. If you are growing Sweet Peas up twiggy branches, the tendrils cling to them and help to support the plants.

### 3. What does chipping Sweet Pea seed mean?

It was always said it is necessary to chip through the hard coat of the Sweet Pea seed in order for moisture to penetrate it. This was always done by nicking through the seed coat with a sharp knife on the opposite side of the eye. On the Sweet Pea seed I have never found this necessary to get good germination with the compost I have already mentioned.

### 4. Can Sweet Peas be grown in a hanging basket?

There is a miniature version of Sweet Pea called Cupid. It is a very dwarf bushy type, very highly perfumed and free flowering. It is ideal for planting in tubs and wonderful for hanging baskets.

### 5. What does layering of Sweet Peas mean?

Sweet Peas grow extremely quickly and can be at the top of an eight-foot cane before the end of July, which means they are difficult to tend. It is necessary to remove all the ties, dropping the Sweet Pea plant from the cane, stretching it along the row and turning it up another cane four plants away. To start with it is necessary to loosen three or four plants to get the layering process begun and then work your way down the full row. Tie the lead plants into their new position and by the end of August they will have reached the top of the cane and flower continuously through the autumn. At ground level it is essential to tie the loose stems with string every two feet; this keeps them tidy and avoids you standing on them.

### 6. I once read it was a good idea to put straw down between the Sweet Pea rows. Is this so?

Many people advocate the use of straw over the soil between the rows of Sweet Peas. This keeps the weed down and helps to keep the moisture in the soil. It also avoids the soil drying out quickly.

### 7. I was always told it was necessary to dig a trench anything up to three feet deep in which to grow Sweet Peas. Is this true?

Sweet Peas make a very long root system and it is necessary to double dig your soil incorporating well-rotted farmyard manure into the bottom spit. If you find the bottom spit is very solid, dig this over with a garden fork which will alleviate the solid base and allow moisture to pass through. I think it is totally unnecessary to dig three feet deep.

### 8. Is there any advantage in growing Sweet Peas in a polythene tunnel or a cold greenhouse?

To get off to a very early start, Sweet Peas grow extremely well under cover. You can be picking Sweet Pea flowers at the end of April from an autumn sowing. It is very necessary as the months go by to give as much ventilation as possible, as overheating can stop the plants from growing. I have been very successful over many years in producing early cut flowers by using my polytunnel and planting in early November. During the growing period inside, never allow the plants to go dry.

### 9. What is the latest sowing date for Sweet Peas?

If sown later than April 12, Sweet Peas do not have time to flower properly before the frost comes.

# Spring Bedding Plants

Most gardens in the winter time lack colour. In order to enjoy spring in the garden, a glorious range of colour can be achieved with a bit of forward planning.

The glorious colours of spring bedding plants – with polyanthus making a major contribution.

# Wallflowers

I think one of the plants that gives you a spectacular display is a member of the cabbage family with not only its vibrant colour but the amazing perfume. Yes – I am referring to the wallflower.

### Propagation

Wallflowers take a long time from sowing to planting out. They are biennial, which means you sow one year to flower the next. In Yorkshire the tried and trusted method is that when your wallflowers in your display are fading and are just past their best, reach for a packet of seed and sow for the following season.

Normally at the end of May or early June I still believe you get the best plants when wallflower seed is sown out of doors in a prepared seedbed. Choose an area of the garden that has not grown any member of the cabbage family for four years. Remember that wallflowers are a brassica. All the cabbage family can get a dreaded root disease called Club Root, which can stay in the soil for fifteen years, so if any member of this family is sown or planted on infected land it will not tolerate it.

I often grow my young wallflowers on land that has grown potatoes the previous year. I dress the soil with lime as wallflowers like a high pH. The seed is sown in shallow drills a quarter of an inch deep.

Sniffing the vibrant perfume of wallflowers.

When the seedlings are about an inch high I water the drill. With a hand fork I then lift out the seedlings in clumps and individually transplant them six inches apart and with twelve inches between the rows. Water the seedlings in well. The important job in the summer is to hoe the beds frequently in order to keep down the weed seedlings. If these were allowed to grow, they would strangle the young plants.

## Soil conditions

When your summer displays are past their best, pull out the plants in late September and dig in some well-rotted farmyard manure. In Yorkshire we are lucky we have plenty of farms with the full range of animals. The excreta from all the farm animals and poultry is excellent. Check the pH and add lime if required.

## Planting out

When your beds are cultivated in September or October, the day conditions are a bit cooler. It is an ideal time to lift the seedlings, which have now grown into bushy plants, and move them into their permanent quarters. My method is to water the seedlings well in their growing quarters the night before you are due to plant. They lift much better when wet. Be careful not to knock all the soil off. Place them in a wheelbarrow and transfer them to their planting quarters. Dig a hole large enough to take the root system and firm in well.

## Varieties

Many people like to see mixed colours:

**Fair Lady Mix:** A wonderful series that contains all the pastel shades and is very highly scented.

**Harlequin Mix:** A superb bedding mixture with a good low branching habit and with rich clear colours.

**Tom Thumb Mix:** Very bushy habit, very dwarf, wonderful for edging off the borders.

**Charity Mix:** A new breakthrough in wallflower growing for flowering in autumn and again in early spring. Small compact plants in an attractive range of colours.

Separate colours:
**Blood Red:** Deep crimson.
**Cloth of Gold:** Rich golden yellow.
**Fire King:** Bright orange.
**Giant Pink:** Rich pink colour.
**Vulcan:** Velvety crimson.
**White Game:** Creamy white.
**Primrose Bedder:** Sulphur yellow.
**Orange Bedder:** Vivid orange.

Charity Mix – a new breakthrough in wallflower growing has an attractive range of colours.

The distinctive deep crimson shade of Blood Red wallflowers.

A fine display of Cloth of Gold wallflowers in Harrogate.

## Joe's Tip

I think it is also a good idea to water young wallflowers as soon as they have been planted. This reduces severe wilting. They will quickly get established, settle down and within a few weeks they will be growing away strongly. On an early April morning, especially if there has been a shower, the perfume will greet you yards away.

# Pansies

There are hundreds of pansy and viola varieties suitable for giving wonderful displays of almost every colour and combinations imaginable.

To get big strong plants to grow through the winter and provide you with an excellent display in the spring, it is necessary to sow the seed in June. But the bonus is they will give you many flowers in late August and in mild winters will flower on and off. During the winter months many people call these winter-flowering pansies. I prefer to call them winter hardy to flower in the spring.

## Propagation

Sow the seed in June or July for planting in September or October. I like to use John Innes No 1 or good multipurpose compost, although now there are composts specially formulated for pansy and viola growing. In a standard-size seed tray I sow about one hundred seeds. The seed is then covered with a fine layer of compost. I normally water the compost before I sow to allow it to drain away.

Try and grow in a temperature to germinate at about 60F. After germination and when the seedlings are large enough to handle, prick out into individual cell trays or three-inch pots. I grow on for a short time in the cold greenhouse. When growing strongly the trays are placed outside to grow on through the summer months.

## Planting out and soil conditions

Normally the pansies are planted where summer bedding plants have grown. I always make sure the soil is well prepared for the summer plants by digging in well-rotted farmyard manure in spring. When the summer bedding has finished, all that is required in the autumn is a dressing of general fertiliser. The soil possibly needs a good watering if it is dry. Planting distance is six to nine inches apart. At this distance plants will fill out without any soil visible.

A healthy-looking bunch of young pansies.

## Varieties

**Dynamite series:** These large-flowering pansies are wonderful. This series contains plants with a compact habit from autumn through until the end of May. There is a full colour range of whites, yellows, reds and blues.

**Beacon series:** Features many bi-colour flowers with the upper petals being a paler version than the lower ones, with a vast range of colours.

**Supreme Ultimate series:** Medium-size flowers with the best winter performance in terms of flowering. In this series many of the colours have a brown blotch in the centre of the petals. My particular favourites are Supreme with yellow blotch, Supreme white with blotch, and Supreme red with blotch.

Massed ranks of the Robella series of Bellis Daisies – noted for their very large flowers.

# Bellis Daisies

Very easy to grow and very winter hardy, Bellis Daisies are a perennial but for bedding purposes they are best treated as a biennial. Sow in June or July in well-ventilated cold frames or a cold greenhouse. Make sure the compost is damp – either a Multipurpose or John Innes No 1 seed compost. Prick into small pots or modules when large enough to handle. They can grow on during the summer in open frames.

### Planting out

Normally from September or October until March, April or May. Same soil conditions as pansies. Good for edging, mass planting in borders, pot containers or baskets.

### Varieties

**Galaxy series:** Small flower types with the advantage of flowering in their first autumn after sowing. Colours range through dark red, light pink and white with yellow daisy-like centres showing.

**Robella series:** Very large flowers with long flat petals. Colours range from rose, red and white to white with red tips.

**Tasso series:** Almost incurved (see photo below).

Colours include strawberry red, pink, deep rose, red and white – and also a mixture of all these colours.

The Tasso series of Bellis Daisies has flowers that are almost incurved.

*Part 3. Floral Glory*

*Polyanthus – one of the showiest of all the spring bedding plants.*

# Polyanthus

The primula polyanthus is possibly one of the showiest of all the spring bedding plants, either planted in separate colours or as a mixture.

## Propagation

The seed can be sown in late spring when the temperature is between 55F and 60F. It must not exceed 65F as this will inhibit germination. Either a John Innes or a multipurpose seed compost must be used – and it is important to keep it moist, cool and shaded. When sowing do not cover the seed with compost. Once the seed has chitted, cover with moist vermiculite to assist rooting for the emerging seedlings . When the seedlings are large enough to handle, transplant into pots or modules for growing on during the summer months. They are best grown in open cold frames without the glass in place and will be ready for planting out in the autumn. Keep the plants well watered during the summer months. It is often necessary to apply a liquid feed during August and September.

## Planting out

It is normal to plant out about the second week of September. In their permanent positions the planting distance is about nine inches apart in both directions. Polyanthus do enjoy moisture-retentive, well-drained soil with a general fertiliser dressing of about two ounces to the square yard. The flowering period extends from early February through until the end of May. Polyanthus often attracts greenfly so it maybe necessary to use an insecticide spray during late April.

## Propagating by division

When polyanthus have finished flowering they can be divided into small sections of individual crowns and replanted in a shady part of the garden. They can then be lifted in autumn and replanted in your flowerbeds.

## Varieties

The Crescendo series is acknowledged to be the finest. It is fully hardy, free flowering and has an excellent colour range. The colours range from blue, red, bright rose, orange and yellow to pink and rose shades, bright crimson and deep salmon with an excellent perfume.

# Garden Auriculas

Hardy auriculas, which were a very popular Victorian bedding plant, are again becoming favoured for colourful spring displays. They are normally sown in a cold frame from February until May on the compost surface and germinate at about 55F maximum. Germination should take between three and five weeks when grown in cool conditions. When large enough to handle, put into small pots and do not over-water. The primula auriculas are a perennial and can also be propagated by taking small offshoots.

## Varieties

**Primula Japonica Auricula Mixed:** The best type.

**Myosotis:** Often called forget-me-not, this is a biennial. Sown in June and July, it will flower in March, April and May the following year.

## Propagation

Sow in a multipurpose compost in trays. When large enough to handle, transplant in modules or small pots. Grow in the summer in open cold frame areas, water frequently and plant out in the autumn in their permanent positions. Forget-me-nots must be one of the easiest bedding plants to grow. They are not fussy about conditions so long as it is well drained and soil retentive.

## Varieties

Everybody thinks forget-me-nots are blue, but nowadays there is a very good colour range.

**Sylva series:** Excellent – and includes Snowsylva (white) and Rosylva (rose pink). Bluesylva is bright blue and has large flowers with tighter-growing flowerheads, producing a fuller plant that shows much more colour.

**Victoria series:** Ball shaped plants that are ideal for mass bedding displays. Varieties are Victoria blue, Victoria rose, Victoria white, Victoria mixed and Victoria lavender.

# Primroses

Primroses are ideal as perennials and can be used either as pot plants or for bedding displays. Propagation is the same as for polyanthus. I think that the Arctic series is the best one for colourful bedding displays in spring and is also very useful in baskets and containers.

## Questions and Answers

*1. Is it necessary to deadhead pansies?*
It is often a good idea to remove the deadheads otherwise the plants will make seedpods to the detriment of the flowering period.

*2. Can we take winter-flowering pansies from cuttings?*
Pansies can be taken from cuttings successfully. Use a non-flowering shoot and cut below a leaf joint. Insert into a sandy compost. Keep out of hot sun while they root, then pot into individual small pots to grow on.

*3. Can we grow pansies from our own saved seed?*
Yes – this can be done successfully but they will not always come true to type. Those from cuttings are exactly like their parents.

*4. Our forget-me-nots self seed all over the garden. Can we transplant these into the borders?*
This can be done successfully but my advice is to plant them when they are very small.

*5. Which is the best place to grow on polyanthus from our own stock that has been split down?*
I find the best place to grow polyanthus for next year's bedding schemes is in part of the vegetable garden in a shady area. Dig in plenty of well-rotted farmyard manure. Transplant the small divided plants in early June about six inches apart and keep well watered. It may be necessary to hoe between the plants in summer for weed control and possibly spray with a systemic insecticide for the control of aphids.

The flamboyant colours of summer bedding plants. Amazing displays can be seen in public parks and town centres.

# Summer Bedding Plants

June, July and August is the time when we see mixtures of magical colours that seem to happen very quickly. The flamboyant colours within the range of summer bedding plants is why they are so popular. Lots of the colour occurs in a short space of time. We can sow plants like marigolds in March and April and they will be in full flower in July. Their colour extends into late autumn, when they are replaced in flowerbeds with the spring bedding plants.

Amazing displays can be seen in public parks and town centres. I think some local authorities do a fantastic job of planting in the streets to bring the radiance of colours to many car drivers and travellers. I have been known to drive twice round a roundabout to see the beautiful colours, but I am a careful driver even in my white van!

In Victorian times, white alyssum was used with blue lobelia as an edging and beds were then filled with Paul Crampel red geraniums. Dot plants like standard fuchsias and standard geraniums were then added.

Dot plants are those that give a focal point to flowerbeds. Schemes can be varied by plants of contrasting colours in the centre of beds – silvers with reds, bronzes with yellows, and so on.

In years gone by all geraniums were propagated by cuttings taken in the autumn and grown on in heat through the winter months. They had to be potted into five-inch pots to keep them growing prior to planting out at the end of May.

These days summer bedding plants often go in the same beds and areas that have grown spring bedding. Before this is planted the ground is well prepared by digging in moisture-retentive material. Summer bedding should therefore just need a dressing of general fertiliser. If the ground is very dry, water well before you plant.

In my lifetime I have grown and planted hundreds of different types. These are many favourites grown and loved not only by Yorkshire folk but by gardeners all over the country:

## Alyssum

Makes a wonderful edging plant. Now comes in many different colours with a lovely sweet perfume. Carpet of Snow, Royal Carpet and Pastel are wonderful varieties that all hug the ground well.

## Lobelia

Requires sowing in a heated greenhouse in February. Groups of about three seedlings can be pricked out into modules and hardened off prior to planting.

## Marigolds

Remarkable series of plants for gardens in the summertime. Plant when all fear of frosts has gone. Watch out for slugs – they love them.

French Marigolds and African Marigolds can be sown in heat in early spring and pricked out into modules, prior to being hardened off in frames prior to planting. The Safari series of French Marigold is the best I have ever grown – and the Inca series of African Marigold is excellent.

## Pansies

Still an all-time favourite. By sowing in a cool greenhouse you will have large plants in full flower in mid-June. Extra good plants can be achieved if grown in individual small pots.

## Violas

Same growing conditions as for pansies.

Dot plants give a focal point to flowerbeds.

A striking bed of the Inca variety of African Marigolds.

Pansies sown in March and photographed at the end of May in an uncovered frame.

*Part 3. Floral Glory*

## Impatiens

We all know this group as Busy Lizzies. Now one of our most popular of bedding subjects.

Sow at 68F in February and March. Do not cover the seed, but press it down into damp compost. When the seed starts to swell, cover lightly with a dusting of vermiculite. Prick off into individual modules or pots. Grow on and harden off prior to planting out.

## Petunias

Magnificent bedding subject. Sow at 65F in March and transplant when large enough into module trays. Plant out end of May.

## Salvias

Blaze of Fire grows very well in Yorkshire gardens. There are some wonderful new varieties and mixtures, whereas once over Salvias were always red. Now the Clover Plant Breeders have created separate series like sizzler with all the different colours.

## Tagetes

Very much like miniature marigolds – and grown in exactly the same way.

## Sunflowers

Loved by everyone. Try Big Smile, only eighteen inches high. Once the first flower has faded many more develop.

## Begonia semperflorens

Care must be taken when sowing. Do not sneeze as the seed is like dust. Sow as for Busy Lizzies. I like the Senator series and President Mixed has all the colours.

## Dahlias

Coltness Mixed make big plants, showy and will fill large areas. Plant about fourteen inches apart. Favourite with northern folk, as you can save the tubers for next year!

# Questions and Answers

*1. I have seen some amazing displays in parks and gardens with a cenre that resembles a large hanging basket. How can I create one?*
It is very easy. Knock a post into the centre of your flowerbed. Make up a large hanging basket and fasten it onto the post. All the trailing plants will hide the post and form a wonderful centrepiece.

*2. Is it possible to save F1 Mimulus seed, as I have had them self-seed in my garden?*
You can save F1 Hybrid seed but they revert back to the original parents and will not come true.

*3. I buy all my bedding plants as young plugs. What is the earliest time I can grow them in my cold greenhouse?*
These plug plants have been grown in ideal conditions. I think April is early enough for a cold greenhouse. On cold nights cover with garden fleece and do not over-water.

*4. I have trouble with my marigolds, which always get stripped. It happens as soon as I plant. Could it be mice?*
No – I think it is more likely to be slug damage. As stated above, they love marigolds.

*5. How do I grow ageratum?*
Sow seed in a propagator in February or March, temperature 60F. Transfer to a cold greenhouse mid-April. Harden off second week in May. Plant out at end of May.

*6. What is the best compost for bedding plants – both sowing and growing on?*
Sow in John Innes seed compost, grow on in John Innes No 1, or use a good multipurpose compost.

*7. What is the feathery-like silver foliage plant used in bedding displays?*
It is Cineraria Silver Dust.

*8. How easy is it to grow geraniums from seed?*
Sow January or February in a greenhouse at 65F. Prick out small plants in pots or modules and grow on until the end of April in heat. Harden off prior to planting at the end of May. Most geraniums for bedding schemes are now grown from seed.

A hanging basket on a post can form an excellent centrepiece to a flowerbed.

**9. Why do we need to deadhead pansies?**
It is necessary to take off flower heads when they have finished flowering to stop the plant making seedpods.

**10. My snapdragons soon go to seed. What should I do?**
When the first flower spikes have finished, nip them off. They will then produce all summer long from side shoots.

**11. What are the best bedding plants to grow near the coast, where we suffer salt spray?**
Mesembryanthemums or Ice Plants make a fantastic display at coastal resorts. They hug the ground well and also enjoy good light intensity.

The distinctive leaves of Cineraria Silver Dust.

Deadheading pansies is a well worthwhile exercise.

119

# Herbaceous Perennials

The definition of a herbaceous perennial is a plant with annual stems and perennial roots. This section of plants is so vast I have picked examples that will give interest during every month of the year.

Lots of perennial plants need support. This is best done by means of a cane, to which the plant can be tied as it develops. Lots of the shorter bushy perennials can be kept upright by placing bushy birch twigs near to the plant. As the leaf stems grow, the twigs keep them tidy and in position.

## Soil conditions

Herbaceous perennials enjoy well-drained, moisture-retentive material. A neutral soil is ideal for most types. Try and get the area weed free.

## JANUARY
### Helleborus niger (Christmas Rose)

This is a hardy perennial that will flower in winter. Soil conditions well drained, with a little shelter. I like the variety Potter's Wheel, which has large bowl-shaped white flowers with green eyes.

## FEBRUARY
### Erysinum (Bowls Mauve)

This perennial wallflower is one of the best plants for flowering all the year round. It can be a short-lived perennial.

## Soil conditions

It likes well-drained soil with a pH of Neutral and over. Plant deeply to the first set of branches and make sure they are firm. There is a tendency for this plant to get badly blown about in wintertime, which can loosen the roots and cause stress. The plant can then be short-lived. I continually root young plants from cuttings before the shoot initiates a flower bud and always have a succession growing on, just in case

Bowis Mauve – a perennial wallflower that is one of the best plants for blooming throughout the year.

I lose one. Having said it is short-lived, I have one that has flowered continuously for five years. What a brilliant plant!

## MARCH
### Bergenia cordifolia (often called Elephant Ears)

The leaves of this plant resemble elephant ears. Large, glossy and deep green, they often turn bright red in autumn and winter. In March and April delightful pink buds appear and develop into very pleasant pink flowers.

## Ground conditions

Not fussy but needs to be well drained. Will thrive quite well in the shade. Watch out in the autumn when leaves are falling from the trees. Pick these off, as wet leaves can rot the evergreen foliage of bergenia.

## APRIL

### Hostas

Hostas are not only grown for their remarkable leaf formations, but certain varieties have flowers with an amazingly sweet scent. They make attractive container plants. This is the month when hostas wake up and spear-shaped buds start to appear. It is the ideal time to propagate, so I lift the plant out of the soil onto a flat surface. With a saw that is past its best, I cut through sections of root with about four growth buds showing. These are then potted into six-inch pots and grown on prior to planting out.

Hostas thrive equally well in sunny positions and shady areas, and in damp soil and dry conditions.

### Best varieties

**Big Daddy:** Huge clump-forming perennial with grey-blue leaves attaining a height of up to a yard.

**Gold Standard:** Heart-shaped yellow-green leaves up to two feet tall with a spread of two feet.

**Hosta Patriot:** Very vigorous perennial. Puckered olive green leaves marked with white and green slashes. Has lavender-blue flowers thirty inches tall. Grows well in pots.

**Vanilla Cream:** Dwarf grower with unusual red dotted leaves. Stalk slightly puckered.

## MAY

### Lupins

A tremendous perennial, although sometimes short-lived, lupins are often classed as a biennial. This means they are propagated one year to flower the next.

Lupins are a wonderful cottage garden subject. The russell varieties have thick and heavy short spikes and are propagated by cuttings. Many of the modern varieties are seed-raised. They are a fully hardy plant, which grows well in reasonably fertile soil or in light sandy soil if it is a bit on the acid side.

Hostas thrive in sunshine and in shade – and have remarkable leaf formations.

Lupins are fully hardy and a wonderful cottage garden subject.

## Propagation

Seed can be sown in spring or autumn to germinate in the cold frame. Watch out for mice – they love lupin seed. Basal cuttings can be taken in spring when the shoots are about four inches long and can easily be rooted in water.

## Varieties

**Noble Maiden:** Creamy white flowers.
**Chatelaine:** Pink and white.
**Chandelier:** Bright yellow.
**Mauve Queen:** Mauve lilac.

## JUNE
## Delphiniums

A wonderful tall plant for the back of the border. They enjoy a sunny position and benefit greatly from good rich land that is moisture retentive. Great care must be taken at spike formation time. The spikes grow very quickly and can often be broken down by the wind. They must be well supported by canes. I tend to tie in individually with raffia or soft string. Delphiniums are at their best when planted in groups of three some thirty inches apart.

## Propagation

An easy way is by cuttings taken in early spring. Using a jam jar, place two inches of sand in the bottom and top up with water. When plenty of white hair roots have been formed, they can be potted in moist compost and grown in the cold greenhouse.

## Varieties

**Black Knight:** Pacific Hybrid type, deep blue flowers.
**Butterball:** Semi-double, light cream.
**Fanfare:** Mauve flowers, very tall grower.
**Guinevera:** Pacific Hybrid type, pale purple flowers.
**Sandpiper:** Semi-double, white flowers.

Apart from having striking colours, delphiniums can also grow so tall that they will need supporting.

## JULY
### Kniphofia (Red Hot Pokers)

At times this plant looks very insignificant. When in flower it resembles a glowing red hot poker straight out of the fire. It will flower from July through to October and can be very spectacular.

An established root can easily be dug out during the dormant period and then divided up and replanted. If you have room, plant in the same way as delphiniums – groups of three thirty inches apart. This will give you colour from midsummer till autumn.

## AUGUST
### Hollyhocks

Old-fashioned hollyhocks in their mixed shades are delightful for a blaze of high colour at the back of the border. People stopped growing them because of a disease called hollyhock rust. My way with rust is to use the spray called Garlic Wonder. I spray frequently in late spring and continue through summer. Natural garlic contains sulphur that helps to combat the disease.

Propagation is by seed and division.

Hollyhocks take me back to Penrith railway station where my dad tended the garden. At the back of it there was a chain-link fence eight feet high and the border must have been eighty yards long. Hollyhocks of all colours were grown against the fence. To keep them upright my dad tied them to the back. In those days there was no sign of hollyhock rust because of the sulphur in the atmosphere from steam engines burning coal. What a spectacular sight as the sun faded in early evening!

## SEPTEMBER
### Astrantia

Innovative breeding has given a new dimension to this old fashioned garden plant with its paper-like flowers. There are yew varieties like deepest red Westfield, red and cream Moulin Rouge, Astrantia Major and Florence, which is lilac. These types are perpetual flowering from June till October.

## OCTOBER
### Grasses

Grasses have become very popular in recent years because of their growth habit throughout the year. They can look splendid even in the depths of winter. Varieties like Gormans Bronze, with its wonderful bronze red foliage, is extremely attractive in the autumn sunshine. Festuca Glauca – with its almost blue-green sheen – can make a stunning feature, especially when planted in groups of three. Briza Maxima, often called quaking grass, is magnificent in October with its tassel flowerheads nodding in the autumn wind. Finally, Melica transsilvanica can be stunning with its red flowerheads sometimes covered with morning dew or a white haw frost.

## NOVEMBER
### Pampas Grass

Pampas grass can give us a new dimension to the garden with its giant plumes showing right through the wintertime. The leaves are very sharp, so make sure you do not catch them with your hand otherwise you can cut yourself. The botanical name for Pampas grass is Cortaderia selloana and one of the best varieties is Sunningdale Silver. Pampas grass enjoys being grown on well-drained and fertile soil in full sun. All dead flowerheads can be removed as they begin to look untidy. Again, be very careful of the razor sharp leaves.

## DECEMBER

Grasses are good right through the winter. This is especially the case when they are mixed in shrub beds or with perennials such as bergenia and cornus.

**Grasses are good even in December.**

*Part 3. Floral Glory*

# Questions and Answers

**1. I remember as a child my mother cutting pyrethrums and putting them in a vase. The flower shops then sold them in bunches. Are they still grown as a cut flower?**

Very rarely do you see these on sale as cut flowers, so it may be necessary to grow them in your own borders. When cut they will last about twelve days in water.

**2. Can delphiniums be grown from seed?**

Blue Fountain, Magic Fountain and Tom Pouce series can all be grown from seed. If the seed is sown in January in a greenhouse, it will flower within six months and then develop into perennials.

**3. What is the best compost to grow lupins from seed?**

I find the soil based compost John Innes No 1 ideal for this purpose.

**4. My lupins get a grey-coloured aphid on them. What is the best cure?**

This is the mealy lupin aphid. Tom in my village has cured the problem for me by putting up some blue tit nesting boxes in my garden. They love aphids, especially when they have youngsters to feed. Tom also makes bird tables and hedgehog boxes – I must remember to take him some fresh vegetables.

The problem of aphids in the garden can be greatly reduced by putting up blue tit nesting boxes. The birds love aphids.

Smilacina Racemosa – ideal for a shady border.

Geums of the Mrs Bradshaw variety photographed in my nursery one year after sowing.

**5. We have a plant in the garden with cream white flowers and dark green leaves. It comes into flower in May. A gardener once told me it was a form of Solomon's Seal. Is he correct?**

I think the plant you have in your garden is Smilacina Racemosa, which is ideal for a shady border.

**6. How do you propagate geums?**

I propagate from seed, often using the Mrs Bradshaw variety.

7. *I would like to grow a perennial plant that I can put in flower arrangements over a long period of the summer. I want it to act as a filler among other summer flowers. What do you suggest?*

Look no further than Lady's Mantle – Alchemilla mollis.

8. *How do I save my dahlia tubers through the winter?*

Dahlias are a tender perennial. They are best dug out of the ground after the first frost, dried in the greenhouse and saved through the winter in a dry frost-free situation.

Dahlias are a tender perennial best kept in a frost-free location through the winter.

Alchemilla mollis, commonly known as Lady's Mantle.

Gunneras – with their huge leaves – thrive on the edge of boggy land.

Despite being classed as a biennial, Sweet Williams can survive for many years.

Coreopis Early Sunrise – one of the easiest perennials to grow from seed.

9. *Can Gunnera manicata be grown in a boggy area?*

This is the ideal situation for Gunneras but they must not stand in water all the time. The fringe of bog land is an ideal location.

10. *Many people say Sweet Williams are a biennial plant but we have them growing year in and year out in the same area. What is the reason?*

Sweet Williams are indeed a biennial, meaning we sow one year to flower the next, but they can then go on for many years to come. I remember my father had a patch of Sweet Williams for at least twelve years.

11. *Can you name a perennial plant that is easy to grow from seed and will flower early in its life?*

Coreopsis Early Sunrise is very easy to grow. Sow the seed in June.

125

*Part 3. Floral Glory*

Keeping a lawn in first-class condition is one of the hardest of horticultural tasks but well worth all the effort.

# PART 4. FINISHING TOUCHES

# Lawns

## Turfing

The quickest way to develop a new lawn is to use turf. Always obtain turf from a reputable turf supplier. The advantage of turfing your area is that you get an immediate lawn that establishes itself very quickly. Do not make the mistake of laying turf without any ground preparation.

### Ground preparation

It is most important to make a good job of preparing your soil for laying turf. I will qualify this by saying once you have a lawn it could easily be there for the duration of your lifetime, so it goes without question that this is a job that should not be rushed. Try to prepare the ground if at all possible many weeks in advance. I would suggest you need at least seven inches of good top soil. If the soil is of a barren nature, it would be an advantage to dig in some organic matter, which will help retain moisture in dry weather conditions. When cultivating your soil, it is essential to remove any large stones and any other debris including perennial weeds.

If your soil is on the heavy side it may be necessary to incorporate some sharp sand. This will open up the soil and make the drainage better. The ideal situation for laying turf is a free-draining soil containing an ample amount of organic matter. If you feel the drainage is going to be poor, you may need to seek advice regarding the laying of land tiles or other such drainage material.

Turf can be laid at any time of the year, but I would advocate not turfing during very hot weather in the height of summer. There again, avoid severe frosty weather, but any mild period during the winter time is ideal.

## Laying turf

It is best to start along a straight side in a row butting tight up to the next row. Continue with the next row and stagger the joints as in brickwork fashion. Always work off planks on the newly laid turf. Make sure there is total contact between the soil and the underside of the new turf. It is a good idea to dress any cracks and joints with fine soil. Apply plenty of water to the newly turfed area. Continue to water until the lawn is established. Any sign of drying out, water it.

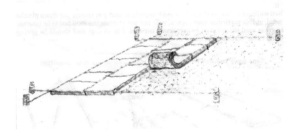

When laying turf ensure that the joints are staggered in the same way as brickwork.

## Lawns From Seed

A seedbed is very important. After all cultivations have been carried out prior to sowing the seed, it is essential to make the soil fine. This can be done by using a wooden hay-rake, which brings the soil down to a fine crumb structure. The preparation of the seedbed is best done on a dry day, when the soil does not stick to your boots. Consolidate the seedbed area by treading it with feet kept very close together. This breaks down the clods, gives the soil the right type of compaction without being too solid and, as I have already said, the final preparation is then done with the hay-rake.

When the preparation has been completed, it is time to sow the grass seed. The easiest way is by emptying it into a bucket and throwing the seed slightly into the air. With being very light, it disperses and gives sufficient space between each seed. Different grass seeds and mixtures probably need sowing at different thicknesses. On average I would say one-and-a-half to two ounces of grass seed to the square yard is adequate.

Prior to buying your grass seed think what type of lawn you are going to make. There are grass seeds for all requirements and most soil types – this is your choice. I will not advocate any particular type of grass seed because all garden conditions and types of lawn you may require are different.

After sowing the grass seed it is necessary to rake it gently in. Do not cover or bury the seed totally. There are two main things which can go wrong at this time. One is the eating of seed by birds; the other is drying out of the surface of the soil prior to the seed germinating. It is most important that the bed be kept moist until the seed has germinated. This will also prevent birds from dusting in the seedbed, thus causing depressions that will make the lawn uneven. After you have spent all the time making a nice even surface this could be destroyed by the birds dusting in the dry soil. Another way to keep the birds off is to criss-cross the area with black cotton; the birds touch the cotton and are frightened by it.

When walking on the seedbed, it is most important that you should put down planks of wood. Again, your feet would cause the bed to be uneven.

The grass seed should start to germinate between seven and fourteen days and should be giving ground cover within a period of twenty-one days.

Consolidating a lawn seedbed by treading the area with the feet. It is important to keep the feet close together.

# Year Planner For The Established Lawn

To keep a lawn looking in first-class condition is probably one of the hardest horticultural tasks. Care and attention all the year round is of the utmost importance and my year planner should help:

### January
Very little work on the established lawn is needed. Clear away any fallen leaves but probably the best thing to do is to keep off the lawn. It is the best time of year to get your lawn mower overhauled and to sharpen your tools.

### February
Again very little work is required. Any worm casts can be scattered with a besom brush or a cane on a dry day, probably towards the end of the month.

### March
Most of the lawn work should begin on a dry day. It is an advantage just to top the lawn, first removing any debris. It is essential to dispel any worm casts before the actual first cut. A cylinder mower should be set high so that the lawn can be just topped; it is essential that early in the year the lawn should not be cut too short as yellowing may happen. Probably only two cuts are required during the month. Beware of the danger of cutting lawns too short in the spring.

### April
Bare areas caused by the winter weather can either be re-seeded or re-turfed. Late in the month seeding and weeding can start. Mow often enough to stop the grass growing away. Do this on a dry day but do not mow too short.

## May

You will need to increase the frequency of cutting – probably once a week depending on weather conditions. When the grass is growing away strongly this is the month to apply selected weed killers, lawn sand, etc. May is often moist enough but if it does turn very hot and dry, do not let the lawn get into a distressed state. Apply water.

## June

Summer frequencies should now be under way with the grass cutting possibly twice a week. Never allow the lawn to become too dry – apply water during dry periods. June is the time for summer feeding and weeding. Keep the lawn edges trimmed right the way through the growing season.

## July

Keep mowing regularly and watering regularly during dry conditions. Use selected weed killer again but only when the lawn is growing strongly and when it is not too sunny.

## August

This is the last month for feeding with a rich fertiliser. Overfeeding at this time of year may result in turf diseases in September and October.

## September

The autumn lawn programme begins in September. You may still need to deter worms because of their casts. Watch out for Fusarium Patch, Dollar Spot and Red Thread. This is the month to do lawn repairs and attend to broken edgings, as the intervals at this time of year are getting longer between each cut. Towards the end of the month get ready to scarify, spike and finally top-dress the lawn. This can go through to October as well. (More about scarifying, etc, under the various lawn headings).

## October

Regular mowing comes to an end. For what may be the last cut, raise the height of the setting on a cylinder mower. Never cut the lawn at this time of the year when it is wet. You can dispel rain and dew with a brush or cane before mowing. Give the edges of the lawn the last trim probably towards the end of October. If you did not scarify, spike or dress the lawn in September get it done in October. I think it is better to do it when the grass stops growing.

## November

You may have to cut the lawn once, but do this with the blades raised. After the last cut give the mower a good clean down and put it away for the winter months. The rest of the lawn equipment wants to be cleaned down before storing. Try and keep any fallen leaves off the lawn.

## December

Remove any fallen leaves. In the event of having to wheel anything across the lawn, make sure that you use boards to prevent rutting.

June is the time for weeding.

If you scalp the lawn in the spring it takes ages to recover. Sometimes it may even need to be re-turfed or re-seeded, so do not cut too short.

*Part 4. Finishing Touches*

# Questions and Answers

**1. What do we mean by scarifying a lawn?**
Scarifying in gardening terms means severely raking the lawn with a scarifyer machine. This has a series of rakes and tines that pull out the moss thatch and dead grasses. This is a great advantage to the grass as it allows it to grow properly. .

**2. We have a lovely dog called Elsie but she occasionally urinates on the lawn which causes discolouration of the grasses. It makes them go yellow and the patches die out completely. How do I deal with this problem?**
I don't know why it is that female dogs cause this problem. Probably it is the way the liquid reaches the grass quickly . Male dogs aim from a higher trajectory so I don't think the problem is as severe. If you are able to spot the mistake happening get a garden fork, spike into the position and drench the area with water. This should dilute the urine and eventually make it work as a fertiliser.

**3. How can I repair areas damaged by dog urine?**
The easy way of repairing lawns after damage has been done is to sow some grass seed in small pots of compost. When germinated and growing strongly, and when the grass seed has filled the pots with root, then cut out the bare areas with a strong knife and plant into that area the pot full of grass seedlings. Firm down with your foot and you have the perfect patch.

**4. What is a springbok rake?**
This is a wire tine rake suitable for pulling out dead mosses, thatch and dead grass. Very useful on small lawns where a motorised scarifyer is not required.

Mr Mole
on his
way.

**5. What is the best time of the year to sow grass seed?**
March, April, September and October are ideal times. This is because the soil is warming up in March and April and there is sufficient moisture at this time of the year. September and October are still ideal as the soil is warm and there is often night time dew and showers to help germinate the seeds.

**6. I want to make a lawn from turf. What is the best time of the year to do this?**
Turf can be laid at any time of the year providing it is not frosty. Avoid mid-summer when the sun is hot and we are in a very dry period. Also try to avoid excessively wet periods.

**7. What is the best time of year to feed the lawn?**
I like to feed the lawn in spring when the worst of the frost has gone, using a spring and summer dressing. This is also followed by a feed say early September with an autumn and winter dressing

**8. I know that wood ash from a wood-burning stove contains potash. Could this be good for the lawn in autumn?**
Many years ago we used to use wood ash on bowling greens in the autumn with wonderful effects. So long as it is neat wood ash, meaning no plastics have been burned, this should be ideal as an organic autumn feed containing potash.

**9. How do I get rid of weeds on my lawn including daisies, dandelions, buttercups and many others?**
One of the best ways is to spray with a lawn weed-killer. The timing is really important because most weed killers are effective when the weeds are growing actively. Always follow the directions on the pack very carefully. If there are only a few weeds they can be dug out by hand or with a trowel.

**10. How do I get nice stripes on my lawn?**
The wonderful effect of seeing nice straight stripes on the lawn is done with careful mowing. The best effects can be achieved by using a cylinder mower with a roller and a grass box that removes the clippings. The striping effect is created by mowing the full length of the lawn and then slightly lapping over the cut area when returning in the opposite direction.

Obtaining straight stripes on a lawn gives a wonderfully pleasing effect.

## 11. What is lawn thatch?

This is the matting together of dead grasses and moss causing a thicket-like membrane, which becomes very difficult for the correct growth of grass. This area ideally should be scarified to break up the thatch, which will result in the healthier growth of the grasses.

## 12. Can I use fresh lawn mowings on my compost heap?

Lawn mowings make a very good form of manure when rotted down. Make sure that when you have applied weed killer to the lawn you do not put the fresh mowings on your compost heap. This is because it can be translocated back into the soil causing damage to plants.

## 13. Can I use fresh lawn mowings to mulch around fruit trees and shrubs to keep down the weeds during the summer times?

It is a good idea to mulch around trees, etc, with lawn mowings, but as in question 12 never use when weed killer has been applied.

## 14. How many cuts after I have applied a dressing of weed and feed fertiliser before I can use the mowings on the compost heap

I would suggest four cuts before you can safely use the mowings.

## 15. I have a problem with moles on my lawn creating havoc. Is it true that using mole cartridges (smokes) will clear the moles away?

Mole smokes can be quite effective when put into the tracks created under the ground. The smoke from the cartridges drives away the moles and hopefully moves them away from lawns. Sometimes the fumes will kill the moles. I believe the most effective method is to trap the moles.

## 16. How do we make an uneven lawn level?

Using a very sandy mixture, carefully fill in the depressions with the back of a rake to level the mixture out. This may take three or four applications as you can only use a fine layer at a time to allow the grass to grow through.

## 17. What is the correct method of using a pair of long-handled edging shears?

To make a perfect straight edge, keep the handle of the shears in your left hand still and use your right hand in a downwards movement. This brings the blades close together making the perfect cut. If you keep both hands moving you often snag the edges and cause a poor finish.

Using long-handled edging shears in the right way is well worth the effort.

*Part 4. Finishing Touches*

# Hedges

There are many reasons why we need a hedge:

*Privacy:* When houses are close together a living barrier can provide privacy and also look good.

*Dividing gardens:* Where a division between plots is necessary a hedge line is very useful and can be kept neat and tidy. It can also be useful for fresh foliage to slip into vases of cut flowers.

*Security:* Very important to many people, so using prickly material like thorn, holly and berberis can work well.

*Shelter:* A good and robust hedge can provide shelter from frost as well as cold and high winds. It is also a haven for birds, especially those that are nesting and feeding on breeding insects. The area beneath a hedge will provide shelter for voles, hedgehogs and the like.

## Ground preparation

This is extremely important as it may be necessary to sustain the plants in the same position for the duration of time spent at the property. When I come to prepare for planting I take out a trench two feet deep and two feet wide, and then break up the bottom by digging in with a garden fork. This should give adequate drainage. Hedging plants do not like their roots submerging in water. It is essential to dig in plenty of moisture retentive material with a good food value. Hedges need plenty of water in dry weather.

If the soil you have taken out of the trench is good, then you can back fill with it. Stones, debris and perennial weeds should be removed.. Try and always start with a clean site, as perennial weeds can prove a problem. Bindweed can choke or even strangle young hedging plants.

## Trimming

When a hedge is immature, trim twice during the growing season. When established, trim once in July (except where otherwise noted below).

Hedges have many functions, such as dividing gardens and giving shelter.

## Types of Hedges

### Beech

Makes a tremendous hedge. Each plant requires 2ft 6in of space. I call it the talking edge because in the winter it retains brown leaves that rustle in the wind and sound like people's voices. This leaf retention also gives extra protection from frost and cold winds.

New leaves fall in early April as the previous year's fall away. I think these new leaves have a green colour that is not present in any other plant. I normally trim off the new growth in late July. This keeps the right amunt of growth during the winter months.

### Holly

A very slow hedge to get established. Planting distance two feet apart. Very attractive and evergreen. With having lots of spiky leaves, holly is sharp and prickly and can be an excellent subject for security. Varieties that have berries can make a stunning feature in winter time. Holly will feed birds in winter and afford shelter in bad weather conditions. Trim with secateurs to avoid chopping through the leaves.

### Privet – gold or green

A dense-forming hedge that can last a lifetime. It can be grown to a good height or kept to about four feet. Most people forget that privet is a growing subject and should be watered well during hot, dry weather. Good strong privet can be trimmed three times from June to September to keep pristine.

### Box

The ideal subject for creating formal gardens. It can be kept very short and regular clipping will maintain it in pristine condition. Planting distance very close, nine to twelve inches apart. Wonderful for planting in shapes to grow roses, tulips and bedding plants. This has been a feature of stately home gardens for hundreds of years – and is now very popular in house gardens. Prepare your area well and dig in plenty of organic matter.

A fine beech hedge giving good protection.

Privet – a dense hedge that can last a lifetime.

Leylandii – a very quick-growing boundary hedge with a bad reputation!

## Quick Thorn Hawthorn

Plant eighteen inches apart. Very quick growing. White flowers in May followed by thornless red berries. Attractive during the winter as the sunshine fades. Provides food for birds in November, December and January. Good as a security hedge.

## Loniceria nittida

A good boundary hedge that can be kept very short and formal. Easy to propagate from cuttings three inches long, taken in April and put into seed trays of a sandy compost. Can be trimmed four or five times a year to look totally formal and perfect condition. Untrimmed loniceria nittida has creamy white flowers followed by purple berries.

## Leylandii

A very quick-growing boundary hedge. Has had a bad press because it can get totally unruly. Keep well trimmed. Spacing wants to be at least a yard apart because of the vigour of the root system. Dig in as much organic material as possible as a moisture retainer. When planting subjects such as leyandii, I like to put a post at each end of the row and attach it to a strand wire to which a cane is fastened. The plant is then tied to the cane to keep it in an upright position. This is important because you can never straighten a maturing plant once it has got established.

Trimming of leylandii should start when the plants are young. This means you can end up with a six-foot high hedge as narrow as nine inches across.

## Common laurel

Planted at least four-feet apart, it makes an informal yet wonderful green barrier with its dense and glossy foliage. An evergreen that needs infrequent pruning.

## Yew

Very slow growing in its early days. Will grow on to make a dense and thick hedge and almost last forever. A good subject as it is quite drought resistant. Most people realise that when growing hedging plants close together the dense root formation quickly dries out the soil. Plant at least four feet apart. Makes a wonderful informal barrier with dense glossy evergreen foliage. Needs infrequent pruning.

Common laurel with its glossy green foliage makes a wonderful barrier.

## Alder

If you have a wet area you may find the alder quite useful, as this fast-growing plant could help to dry it. Has yellow catkins followed by purple seed cones, which the birds will find attractive to eat during the winter. Planting distance 2ft 6in.

## Hornbeam

One of the well-known hedges of yesteryear now making a comeback. It has the great feature of retaining its old leaves during winter time. They fall off as the new leaves come in May. This makes a good hedge for privacy. Fifteen plants will create a five-yard row. From plants 2ft 6in in height you should have a hedge six to seven feet high in five years.

## Mixed Hedges

The mixed hedge can add a new dimension to a garden and is becoming a very popular feature, as people are using them as a background to a border. For example, if you were designing a perennial border the mixed hedge line not only gives the height but also adds colour and interest at different times of the year. It is very much an informal hedge and is often left untrimmed. The individual subjects can however be trimmed after flowering. Below are three plants that will combine together to give good association in a mixed hedge. You can also mix some of our traditional hedge plants among them.

### Rosa rugosa

Almost the wild rose in its own right, it will give you a thorny barrier. Glossy green foliage and perfumed flowers. The bonus is the orange hips in the autumn.

### Forsythia

Adds a blaze of yellow flowers in February and March. The height it attains will add great stature at the back of the hedge line. Cut out a third of the older flowering growth each year. This will encourage new growth to develop and flower the following year.

### Berberis thumbergii atropurpurea

Has purple red leaves and yellow flowers with lots of prickly thorns. If as part of the hedge you need to plug a gap with something spiky, this berberis and the rosa rugosa will keep any one out.

After a slow start, yew will grow to make a dense and thick hedge.

The distinctive purple-red leaves of Berberis thumbergii atropurpurea.

135

# Questions and Answers

*1. I always have White Fly on my beech hedge. What should I do?*
A good cure for whitefly is to spray frequently with a systemic insecticide to stop the life cycle.

*2. Can we use hedge trimmings on the compost heap?*
Hedge trimmings can be used, but do not put them in dense layers. If you use some well-rotted manure among the trimmings this will aid the rotting process.

*3. Do roses make a good hedge and, if so, what is a good variety?*
Queen Elizabeth, tall growing and with a pink flower, makes a stunning hedge.

*4. In many large gardens I have seen a climbing plant with red flowers growing through the top of the hedge. It is extremely attractive. What could it be?*
The plant is Tropaeolum speciosum, often called the flame creeper or the flame nasturtium.

*5. Can I grow holly plants from seed for a hedge?*
Holly berries are very useful but quite slow to form new plants. Pick off the ripe berries in January. Insert them into pots of sand, which should be left outside in the cold wet weather. Bring them into a warm greenhouse in April and watch them germinate. Then plant into small pots of compost. It takes two years for them to reach planting size.

*6. How do I propagate my own privet cuttings?*
Use material that is two years old. Cuttings need to be twelve to fourteen inches long and taken in October. Insert them into a trench in the open garden. It will take about six months to root.

*7. Why does my leylandii hedge turn brown?*
Often this is due to the soil being very dry under the hedge because of the canopy not allowing water to reach it. It could also be an attack of red spider mite or conifer midge.

*8. Do you know of something unusual that would make a nice barrier hedge line?*

Laurel leaf after an attack by adult vine weevil.

Yes – plant Photina Red Robin alternately with Acuba, which is a spotted laurel. This is a very striking combination.

*9. We have a laurel hedge. When do we prune it?*
I think the best time is early April.

*10. Our laurel hedge gets mildew. How can we cure it?*
Your laurel hedge needs spraying in early spring with a systemic fungicide at monthly intervals. Also make sure you water in dry weather conditions to avoid stress, which can bring on an attack of mildew.

*11. Leaves on our laurel get eaten from the outside edge. What could be doing it?*
Vine weevil adults feed on tough leaves like laurel.

*12. Why does our privet hedge looks thin and weak?*
Privet hedges often become very weak because we very rarely think to water them. Privet makes a dense fibrous root system, which dries the soil out to a fine crumb structure. It is a good idea to mulch around the hedge when the soil is wet. This will suppress the moisture into the soil.

**13. When I bought my box hedging I noticed there were three plants in a six-inch pot. If I planted these would my hedge get too congested?**

Growers of box hedging will often put three into a pot to give the illusion of a larger plant. If this is spotted, re-pot singly and grow these on. They will make stunning plants.

**14. My path is close to my hedge. When we have snow, I move it onto the border and place it among the hedge's plants. Can this do any harm?**

This is a really good idea with hedges such as privet. As the snow slowly melts it will give a good drenching to the soil below. The only time we don't put snow on the borders is when we have used salt to thaw it, as this inhibits growth.

**15. When mowing my lawn could I use the cuttings to mulch around the hedge plants?**

This is a very good idea. Do not use a very dense layer at one application as the cuttings heat up and could burn the hedge roots. Never use grass cuttings if herbicide has been applied to the lawn to kill weeds.

**16. Does snowberry make a good hedge?**

It makes a wonderful hedge and can thrive very well on poor soil and be tolerant of exposed sites. Its botanical name is Symphorcarpos. The best variety for hedging is called white hedge, with an upright habit with large white fruit.

**17. Do hedges need watering and feeding?**

Yes, yes – people never think of feeding and watering hedges. We must remember that hedges consist of growing plants, which we place very close together to make a barrier. The amount of root development beneath the surface is quite vast, so we need to water and feed.

# Shrubs

Shrubs can give you a spectacular backdrop to a garden. In general terms most types are very hardy with tremendous flushes of colour during the flowering period. Other shrub material can give you very colourful bark during the months of the year when flowers are scarce.

Some shrub types can provide a fantastic show of berries, especially in autumn, winter and early spring. Others are grown for their attractive variegated foliage, especially in winter. One other important feature is that some shrubs are useful to cover unsightly buildings. These types are useful because of their climbing ability.

Most shrubs like good deep soil.

There are so many thousands of shrubs that I have selected twelve types plus varieties for year-round interest.

## JANUARY
### Hamanellis Mollis

One of the most unusual shrubs for garden use. Its common name is Witch Hazel. Spider-like flowers on bare stems with a fantastic perfume. Needs a well-drained moisture-retentive soil, on the acid side. This plant really is a winter wonder.

Normally grafted. Can also be seed raised but with variable results.

*Varieties*
**Pallida Sulpher:** Yellow, highly scented.
**Hammulis Diane:** Red to orange flowers.
**Hamamlles Brevettila:** Small yellow petals, good scent.

The distinctive spider-like flowers of Witch Hazel have a fantastic perfume.

*Part 4. Finishing Touches*

## FEBRUARY
### Forsythia

I say the herald of spring is the snowdrop. The next one must be forsythia. Suddenly from the desperate depths of our cold, wet and miserable days, yellow blooms appear over garden walls. We probably have not noticed the swelling buds all winter waiting for better light and a little more warmth. Forsythia grows very slowly through the winter time waiting for spring.

We always have forsythia in our house on Christmas Day in full bloom. I cut some tightly budded twigs the first week in December, bring them indoors, put them on the window sill in a vase in a warm room with plenty of water, and watch them come into flower.

The flowers will last until well into the new year and then suddenly leaves will appear. Leave these in the water and roots will start to form. At this stage they can be taken out of water and potted into compost placed in a cold greenhouse and by late spring you will have a forsythia plant to put in your garden.

## MARCH
### Vinca Major Varigata

A grow-anywhere plant with evergreen variegated foliage that loves the shade. I have selected this as my March plant but by no means does it stop there. It can still be seen at its best in autumn.

Blue flowers on yellow-green variegated leaves. Fantastic ground cover. Place three plants a yard apart for total ground cover in just one year. Put daffodil bulbs with it for a stunning carpet.

Propagate by digging up rooted slips and replant – it is just as easy as that.

## APRIL
### Tamarisk

Will give interest in the shrub garden from April till July. Their feathery green fern-like foliage is followed by stunning plumes of pink flowers that are decidedly delicate. Yet they are one of the toughest of all shrubs. They survive drought well and are one of the best plants to grow in seaside regions as they can tolerate sea spray better than any other shrub.

Berberis darwinii has attractive orange-yellow flowers in dense clusters.

### Berberis Darwinii

The whole range of berberis is a tremendous family. They are all quite thorny, so care must be taken where you plant, especially where young children are concerned.

Berberis darwinii is an evergreen with leaves shaped like a duck's foot or a small holly leaf. It flowers tremendously well each May and is followed by attractive berries in the autumn. Birds find it useful in winter time, scratching through the leaves at the base of the shrub to pick up fallen berries. It has attractive orange-yellow flowers in dense clusters. Plants can be kept in check by selective pruning or allowed to grow into spectacular specimens. In my opinion this is one of the finest of the spring-flowering shrubs.

Berberis darwinii can be propagated from seed in early spring. You can root softwood cuttings in early summer in a shady greenhouse. Keep the cuttings moist until rooted and then place individually into small pots using a sandy compost. When large enough they can be planted into permanent positions.

Kerria japonica will brighten up
any corner of the garden

Mock Orange (Philadephus) is a hardy shrub. It thrives
in the garden of this book's editor, 800 feet up in the
windswept Pennines.

## MAY
### Kerria Japonica

I have selected this very popular shrub as it flowers in
May. It is such a useful subject as it can be planted as
a wall shrub and also in a very large container say as
big as a dustbin. It has such a bright colour it will
brighten up any corner of the garden. It is a hardy
plant enjoying full sun or partial shade. The soil
conditions need to be well drained and it prefers rich
land.

I find the best way to propagate is by dividing up
shoots in autumn with roots attached and putting
them into pots for planting in the following spring.
Green shoot cuttings can be taken in early summer.

## JUNE
### Philadelphus

Mock Orange is the common name for Philadelphus.
If you require a plant that will give you fantastic
perfume then look no further. It blooms profusely
during June and July with stunning flashes of white
and cream flowers. It can be kept in check by pruning
about a third of the older flowering stems immediately
after flowering has finished. Philadelphus is fully hardy
and will grow very well in most conditions as long as
the soil is well drained. It enjoys full sun but will thrive
quite well in partial shade.

Propagate by taking softwood cuttings in summer
or hardwood in autumn and winter.

I particularly like the variety Philladelphus virginal.

## JULY
### Buddleia

Every garden should have a buddleia. Dramatic and
easy, it can be pruned down to about six inches from
ground level in February or March. The flowers are
born on the new growth, which is promoted very
quickly. Watch the butterflies arrive when it flowers
between July and September. They love this shrub,
which is also known as the Butterfly Bush.

Propagate by hardwood cuttings in November.

*These are some of the best of the many varieties:*
**Black knight:** Has dark purple-blue flowers.
**Buddleia davidii:** Can flower from early summer to
late autumn. The highly scented purple flowers are
often twelve inches long. This is the real Butterfly
Bush.
**White harlequin:** Sweetly scented with creamy
white flowers.
**Pink delight:** Twelve inches long. Bright pink
flowers with orange splashes in them.
**Royal red:** Unusual dark red to purple flowers often
up to eighteen inches long, stunning in colour.
Propagate by hard wood cuttings in November.

*Part 4. Finishing Touches*

## AUGUST
### Hydrangea Hortensis

The big mop-head forms of hydrangea are breathtaking. Easy to grow, although they enjoy well-drained moisture-retentive material that is a bit on the acid side. Most people leave the old flowerheads in place during the winter. This does protect the small embryo flower buds for the coming year. They can attain a height of six feet but by good pruning this can be reduced. Be careful, as next year's flowers can easily be pruned away. These are fully hardy plants and will thrive in partial shade. The dried flowers can be used in winter arrangements,

Hydrangea can suffer from powdery mildew, honey fungus, aphids, red spider mite, vine weevil and capsid bugs.

Propagation is by rooting softwood cuttings of deciduous hydrangea in early summer or hardwood in winter. It is best when rooting cuttings to use non-flowering shoots.

## SEPTEMBER
### Caryopteris Summer Sorbet

This is one of the newer garden plants and can be of great interest from July till late September. Its dwarf growing habit is very attractive, especially in late spring, with its wonderful variegated foliage. It grows about a metre high and is an extremely bushy shrub. It is pest free. Keep well watered during hot dry periods.

## OCTOBER
### Berried shrubs

This is the month when we can enjoy all the wonderful coloured range of berried shrubs. A good example:

**Callicarpa profusion:** Best planted in groups of three to give you maximum impact with 2ft 6in between each plant. Lilac flowers in summer and pinkish foliage in September followed by lilac-coloured berries In autumn. Cut back hard in February when the berries have gone to give you bushy plants for the next season.

## NOVEMBER
### Cornus Alba

You can rely on the cornus family for midwinter colour when everything else has lost its leaves. Its

Cornus alba comes in several varieties, which differ markedly in appearance. Here are Cornus alba with its distinctive red stems and the green form (Cornus alba siberica).

colourful bark is enhanced by the colder winter weather. Can be planted as one specimen or in groups of three. The common name is Dog Wood and it is grown for its bark (joke!). It is not really all that fussy but soil needs to be well drained. Cut back to six inches from ground level in April as the newly promoted growth gives you enhanced bark colour.

Propagation is by cuttings taken in November and inserted into the open ground.

Varieties include:

**Cornus alba siberica:** Green in form.

**Cornus alba midwinter beauty:** Orange yellow-skin.

**Cornus alba:** Red stems.

## DECEMBER
### Cotoneaster Cornuba

Very vigorous semi-evergreen shrub or tree with white flowers borne in July. In my opinion this is the finest of all the berry shrubs. Two varieties are:

**Cotoneaster hybridus:** Pendulus and forming a small shrub with weeping branches when grown as a standard. Dark green leaves and bright red berries.

**Cotoneaster dammeri:** A very vigorous prostrate evergreen shrub that gives wonderful ground cover. Has white flowers in July followed in the autumn by red berries. The white flowers are borne solitary, and the berries are spherical in shape.

# Questions and Answers

**1. How and when do we prune forsythia?**
Prune immediately flowering has finished by removing a third of the old flowering wood.

**2. Which is the cotoneaster I can use as a wall shrub?**
Cotoneaster horizontalis. It is often called the herringbone cotoneaster because the branches are reminiscent of the bones of this fish. When planted against a wall it is self-supporting. Pink flowers in the spring are followed by many hundreds of red berries in autumn and winter.

**3. Can Kerria japonica be grown against a wall?**
It is growing well against a wall of a shed in our garden. Flowers well in May, June and July. With its orange flowers it really stands out.

**4. Can you name a shrub that can flower through the winter and hopefully give perfume?**
Viburnum X. Bodantense. The variety Dawn has dark pink flowers sometimes paling to white and has a delightful scent. It likes good soil that is well drained and is brilliant for woodland garden or in a shrub border.

**5. What is the best time to cut an old lavender back in North Yorkshire?**
In Yorkshire I would suggest early April.

**6. What is a low-growing shrub that will give ground cover in shade?**
Pachysandra terminalis will cover the ground even in fairly dense shade. It has a white flower on evergreen foliage from February to April.

**7. Are Pernettya berries poisonous?**
Pernettya berries are not poisonous and are enjoyed by birds.

**8. Can you name a blue hydrangea?**
I have grown Hydrangea You and Me Together Blue, which is a very god variety.

**9. I would like to plant an evergreen shrub to flower in**

The dark pink flowers of Viburnum X. Bodatense.

winter and spring against a wall. What would you suggest?
Garrya elliptica, which has large grey-green catkin-like flowers from late November until the end of March, is very suitable for planting against a wall.

**10. I often see a shrub with young and very bright red leaves in April. Can you name it?**
I believe this is Photina red robin.

**11. We would like to plant red, blue and pink rhododendrons. Can you advise good varieties that are not too vigorous?**
Scarlet Wonder is an excellent red, Bluetit a compact blue and then there is Pink Drift. These are all dwarfs.

Scarlet Wonder rhododendron. This plant, growing in Ilkley, is fifteen years old.

*Part 4. Finishing Touches*

**12. Is there such a plant as a weeping rosemary? I have the ideal place in my herb garden.**
Rosemarinus officinalis capria. This is an evergreen herb or weeping shrub with blue flowers and a ground cover habit.

**13. When is the correct time to prune my snowball bush Viburnum opulus?**
It is best pruned after flowering has finished.

**14. I live very close to the sea and most shrubs suffer. Can you name a shrub that will tolerate salt spray?**
Tamarisk is one shrub that does well in coastal areas. It is very tough and will tolerate both salt spray and drought (see page 138).

**15. My skimmias have lots of yellowing leaves. Could they be short of something in the soil?**
Skimmias suffer from magnesium deficiency that causes leaves to yellow. Epson's Salts will do the trick with two teaspoonfuls to a gallon of water.

**16. I need a contrast at the back of my shrub border. Are there two shrubs from the same family and of similar height that will provide this for me?**
Sambucus nigra black lace and Sambucus sutherlands gold, respectively with deep purple and vivid yellow foliage, should give the perfect contrast.

**17. What is the best time of year to move shrubs in the garden?**
In general terms any mild period between mid-November and mid-March is ideal.

# Rock Gardens

A well-built rock garden can be a fantastic feature. However, during my life in horticulture I could count on one hand the rock gardens that have pleased me. Lots of people think a heap of topsoil, with stones, bits of concrete or bricks set into it, is a rock garden.

My idea of a rock garden is a feature that in miniature can depict a rigid section of a mountain. When finished and planted it should be dressed with shale or scree of the same type of stone used to build it. One or two outcrops placed in the foreground can lead your eye up to the rock garden. It is all about creating an illusion. Yes – a mountain in miniature displaying the correct plants.

When sighting your rock feature choose the right location. Many people put the rock garden in a position where nothing else will grow, for example under trees, under hedges, between houses or in shade or poor light. Wet areas are also favoured in the mistaken belief that the elevation of the rocks might improve drainage of the planting crevice. It is not realised that the root formation will eventually be stood in water. Nine times out of ten, a rock garden built in a poor location will quickly end up being an eyesore.

### Design and construction
When designing your rock garden it should ideally fit into the surrounding area in harmony with all other features in the vicinity. This might not be possible in a small town garden that lacks proper landscape features. If this is the case it can act as a focal point, so if it is well constructed it will not hurt your eye.

I have seen brilliant rock gardens built all over the country from the Lake District to Devon and of course in 'God's Own County' of Yorkshire. Here we have limestone, sandstone and millstone grit – I could go on! I think it is wonderful to use local stone for your rock garden features, as has been done with limestone at Harlow Carr gardens in Harrogate.

When I first started building rock gardens I spent hours looking at formations in the Yorkshire Dales. Most of my inspiration came from here, but in recent years I have spent more time close to home at Almscliffe Crag.

There is a very good way to practice rock craft. If in a large tray, get some small pieces of rock, some soil and have a go. It is a good way to spend a wet day – indoors!

Almscliffe Crag, between Leeds and Harrogate, is noted for its outcrops of millstone grit. These are a source of inspiration when planning a rock garden.

Effective use of limestone at Harlow Carr gardens in Harrogate.

## Building a rock feature on a slope

A sloping area of land lends itself to outcrops of rock. Within this area it will be necessary to form steps for access. These should be constructed of the same type of stone and scree, although I have seen excellent steps made of logs infilled with pebble or scree. The outcrop rocks are butted up together with the strata facing the same way. Lots of rocks have natural fissures and cracks in their formation, so try and fit them with the cracks at the same level. This creates the illusion of natural cracking on a rock face – an attention to detail that gives the feature a master's touch.

## Building on a flat site

A flat site is very demanding. The way I have always started is to work from the front, creating the first layer and then back filling with good clean soil. Ram the soil in well around the rocks and avoid straight lines as this looks like a wall. Look out for rocks with crevices as these are ideal situations for plants.

*Part 4. Finishing Touches*

Juniper communis compressa is a magnificent dwarf conifer for rock features and scree gardens. This specimen is twenty-five years old.

I select a key stone, which I place as a feature prominent to the eye and in the centre of the first line or strata. Place the next stone touching the back shoulder, as this avoids straight lines. If you get the first rock wrong you will have a difficult build.

## Planting a rock garden

Never be in a hurry to plant up the newly built rock feature. Soil should be allowed to wash in and settle around the rocks. After a period of time it may be necessary to top it up. Weed control is very important, so be careful when bringing in soil. It can contain many thousands of weed seedlings, which germinate readily during April and May. Again when choosing your soil, be very careful that it does not contain roots from perennial weeds such as mare's tail, bindweed, docks and wick grass or twitch (also commonly known as couch grass). If these get established under the rocks they are extremely difficult to eradicate.

House leeks are highly suitable for rock gardens – and especially for planting in cracks and crevices.

Opposite: Many types of primula fit into damp areas on the edge of rock features.

## Soil conditions

In general terms most rock garden plants thrive on really well drained conditions. I like to add plenty of grit sand to the soil. This allows alpines and rock garden plants to enjoy good drainage facilities. It is often a good idea to make individual planting stations in your rock garden. For example, remove a bucketful of soil and backfill with a mixture that will suit the individual plant. Some plants like acid conditions and others alkaline, so you can suit all needs by preparing in this way.

## Stone troughs

Fantastic miniature rock gardens can be made by using authentic stone troughs. Original stone troughs are very sought after and can cost many hundreds of pounds. They are best planted up with choice alpine types and selected miniature bulbs where the soil mix can be made to suit the needs of the specific plants.

Some people like to convert a greenhouse into an alpine house so that choice plants can be grown to perfection. A brilliant example is at Harlow Carr, where the new alpine house opened in 2010.

Try and make sure all troughs have got drainage holes in them, otherwise plants will die off due to waterlogged conditions. A small hollowed-out stone trough can look a picture when planted with sedums, house leeks and sempervivum. Avoid growing vigorous plants like aubretia in troughs as they can overwhelm other plant material.

Original stone troughs can look magnificent, but they can also cost a fortune.

Interior and exterior of the new alpine house at Harlow Carr, Harrogate.

Aubretia is a very free-flowering plant for the larger rockery. It should be avoided in stone troughs as it can overwhelm other plants.

A small hollowed-out stone can look wonderful if carefully planted.

# Gardening Friends
# I have known

## Eddie O'Donnell

I have got to start this chapter about my garden friends with a wonderful man called Eddie O'Donnell. Eddie was a brilliant grower of vegetables on an allotment site on the Gipton Estate in Leeds. He was a very dedicated person, and if he set his mind to something it would happen. He was also one of the kindest people you could meet.

When I was a young man in Leeds I would go to shows and would marvel at the giant onions, leeks and so on. Always coming first and with his name everywhere was Eddie O'Donnell. I started showing my vegetables at local shows, each year trying a larger one. I went to Shadwell Show in early August, and decided I was good enough to show a collection of vegetables. I loaded my car, took black cloth to form a stage and set up my collection. There were three other collections in the class but when I took a step back to look at them I was happy with my effort.

Just as I was about to leave, a very small man came in, looked at my effort and said, "Well done young man." There was a space next to mine, and he put some black cloth down and some empty dishes with sand, two paper plates and some cardboard rings. When I returned in the afternoon Eddie had done the business. He had erected a stand with

two blanch leeks in beautiful condition, six giant onions, six beautiful tomatoes, six Vanessa potatoes, two celery and the best cauliflowers I had ever seen. He absolutely took me to the cleaners and thrashed me out of site.

Later in the afternoon we talked. He was still pleased with my exhibits and apparently I was closer to him than anyone in recent years. This is when I realised I was talking to a true gentleman. Eddie invited me to his garden to show me his methods. There were no secrets. He then said I had to go and see him next April and he would grow me fifteen leeks, fifteen onions, fifteen celery, twenty cauliflowers and six Shirley tomato plants.

When I went to see Eddie I took him my father's strain of pea, six Bishop potatoes, some long carrot seed and some parsnip seed. I had prepared for my gifts from Eddie, got them planted and tended them well.

Months later in the tent at Shadwell I staged my collection and to keep it fresh I covered it over with a cloth. Eddie's vegetables

**Five-foot high Eddie O'Donnell and I (when I had hair!) at our stand at Harrogate Show in 1980.**

*Part 4. Finishing Touches*

grew very well for me and I was pleased with my effort. I finished early because I was on my way to another show. On my way out of the tent, Eddie came in and we said we would meet in the afternoon. To my great delight I scored one more point with my collection than did Eddie and got the Red Card.

When we met in the afternoon he shook my hand and with great emotion said, "Very well done Joe." I then realised I had a friend for life, so I called him 'The Little Big Man'. He was about five feet tall with a heart as big as a giant.

In the individual classes he beat me with the peas, potatoes and carrots that I had given him to grow and I beat him with the leeks and onions that he gave me to grow. Eddie and I never ever showed against each other again.

Years later in 1980 we set out to grow for a large exhibition stand at Harrogate. Eddie grew the specimens on his allotment and I grew mine on a plot of land near to my house. We were excited and our planning was good. Harrogate Show came and we borrowed a horse box to convey all the produce. Judging was on Friday morning at 7am. Our plan was to work late on the Thursday night – and we were just sweeping up and finishing when the judges arrived. It had taken us all night and we were shattered.

I had also been booked to judge all the local classes at 7am that morning. I don't know how we managed but we did. Then it was a full day on the stand, talking all the time. But to our great delight we won the large gold medal.

Left to right: Tom Agar, Geoffrey Smith and I at York Gate on February 9th, 2002 – a truly memorable day when I became the 'unpaid godfather' to this wonderful garden.

## Summoned to York Gate

One Wednesday morning a few years ago I received a telephone call from a wonderful gentleman and horticulturist called Tom Agar. Tom was renowned in the Yorkshire area for his amazing knowledge on any subject to do with gardening.

The call was an invitation – or rather a summons – to go to York Gate garden, Leeds. It is one of the best small gardens in the world – only an acre but a real gem. The call was something along the following lines. Tom said, "9-30 Saturday morning. Whatever you are doing, cancel it. York Gate 9-30, don't be late. Geoff Smith will be with me." Geoffrey Smith was a great friend of mine and I think possibly the best TV gardener.

Saturday morning came. Now on Saturday mornings in February my nursery is very busy because I stock about a hundred varieties of potatoes. People come early to get certain varieties before they are sold out. So I was a little late and got a slight rollicking from Tom – but only slight. Then Tom said, "Put your arm straight out, palm of the hand open." Next he clasped my hand and Geoffrey put his hand on top of mine.

Tom said, "It's yours now Maiden."

I replied. "Mine – what are you talking about?"

It transpired I had now become the unpaid godfather to York Gate. I am there to safeguard its upkeep and to rally people. If anyone says, or does anything wrong to do with this wonderful garden, I have to put them right.

This is a magnificent garden, which was started by Sybil Spencer. Tom Agar had a lot to do with the right plant for the right place. The garden is now owned by Perennial – the Gardeners' Benevolent Society. The Head Gardener is David Beardall, who does a remarkable job.

York Gate today. It is still one of the best small gardens in the world.

## Gerry and Terry

I am proud to say I was a friend of Gerry Thompson and was honoured to say a few words at his funeral. I could have gone on for hours. The things he had done included book-binding, stamp collecting, growing auriculas, pansies and gooseberries, acting as an allotment shed manager and many more.

Terry Kent would pick Gerry up in his car on Friday mornings at 6.30. They arrived at my nursery at 7.15 and we would put the world to rights over a cup of tea. Then we would start work, which was of course unpaid. Terry did the sowing – and still does. Gerry did the potting and was very good at it.

Like me, Terry is not a true Yorkshireman but he is still working towards it. A wonderful friend, he still comes on Saturdays to sow my vegetable seedlings. Where would we be in life without friends you can trust? He is very articulate and sows in straight lines. His wife Wenda knows my weakness and sends me sweeties.

**Terry Kent (left) and Gerry Thompson.**

## John Smiles and David Allison

A top grower and professional horticulturist with lots of knowledge, John works with rhubarb, strawberries, cauliflowers and other vegetables. The only one thing wrong with John is that he is a Sunderland fan. He keeps reminding me of their Wembley win against Leeds United. John is treasurer of the West Yorkshire Branch of the National Vegetable Society.

David Allison, editor of the National Vegetable Society's newsletter, is always in a hurry and yet can grow everything – not bad for an ex bank manager!

## Mr Jim & Mrs Jim Naylor

I first met Mr Jim at Leeds Horticultural Society. What a man of stature! He was our chairman, a brilliant rose grower, took no prisoners and did not suffer fools gladly. Over the years Jim, who I admired greatly, became a good friend and set up for me the rose section at the Great Yorkshire Show. I was manager and tried my hardest to get rose trade stands to the show. My last resort was to ask Jim to bring in the amateur rose growers. He did me proud and to me the show goes on in Jim's memory.

Mrs Jim is a wonderful rose grower and exhibitor in her own right with top Red Cards behind her. She is a lovely lady with a lovely laugh.

## Alan Talbot

Alan is now chairman of the West Yorkshire Branch of the National Vegetable Society. I am his vice-chairman – an easy Job for me as he is so good. Tim Crowther, who presents our garden programme on Radio Leeds, enjoys Alan's regular contribution. On the preceding Sunday, he tells everyone about the speaker at the next Vegetable Meeting on the second Tuesday of each month. It is held at 8pm at Leeds Paxton Hall, near the Headingley Cricket Ground.

## David Lister

I admire David greatly for his services to such bodies as the Royal National Rose Society. He had one of the best rose nurseries in Yorkshire. There is also his life's work for Leeds Horticultural Society, where he has done every job. He still does, and even opens his house for the meetings. His wife Sheila is always dead on time with tea and biscuits.

The society continues to go forward and its show is now held at Leeds Grammar School in early August, guided by the chairman Elizabeth Bidgood.

## Jim and Old Jim Smith

What a pair! Old Jim, who sadly is no longer with us, was a remarkable and lovely character. He was chairman of the Leeds & District Gardeners Federation. Young Jim told me that one day his dad took some of his Howgate Wonder apples off his tree to put in a show. However, the show was three weeks away. He put them in the freezer and duly showed them on the Saturday. He won first prize, but by the time the show opened in the afternoon they had thawed into a wet mess with water everywhere.

Young Jim, my really good friend, knows a bit about everything and is always there to help.

Anne, one of the best transplanters I know, has also often come to help when I am in a mess. She can be relied on to make some excellent cakes and puddings.

## Gordon and Shirley Kirby

Last but not least, there is Gordon Kirby. He was at Temple Newsam Park in Leeds all his working life and was manager for over thirty years, becoming a brilliant grower of chrysanthemums, tomatoes, cauliflowers and coleus. Temple Newsam claims to be the largest park in Europe. When Gordon was there, they set up many national collections of plants and maintained a high standard. This especially applied to the famous Rhododendron Walks in May and June.

Gordon and I have been colleagues and friends since I started working for Leeds Parks a hundred years ago – only kidding! Gordon is chairman and Shirley secretary of Leeds Horticultural Society. It meets at St Chad's Centre in Headingley on the first Tuesday each month. I co-chair the meetings but it is easy with a partnership like that of Gordon and Shirley. Gordon's humour is very dry and when he starts a tale, he goes on a bit. Then suddenly the punch line – and we all crack up!

# Old Joe Maiden

**M**y father was an amazing chap. He had been a railway man most of his life but I remember him telling me about the early days of his working life. He then worked at the local church for the parson, who had a very large garden at the vicarage. One day, when it was very hot, my Dad stuck his head under the spout of the pump well to cool down. The old parson came around the corner and said to Dad, who was still dripping wet, "Don't work too hard!" The parson thought he was sweating but Dad did not make him any wiser.

Dad was born in Surrey, but spent his early days in Shropshire. His father was a head huntsman for one of the royal hunts. The family had a background in hunting and my father's grandfather is talked of in a book called the *Green Collars*. There are many passages on the 'Fearless Huntsman' known as Peg Leg Joe Maiden, who lost his leg by falling into a vat of boiling dog food for the hounds. Apparently, he just put some wrapping around the scald and carried on making sure the hounds were fed! Eventually his leg was removed and a peg leg made in America especially for him was fitted. The legendary Peg Leg Joe continued hunting.

My Dad was a wonderful gardener and used to win many prize vegetables and flowers. His favourites were Wallflowers Sweet Peas and Roses, all of which were highly scented. I remember as a small boy helping Dad to dig the Sweet Pea trench in the back garden. It seemed to be enormous – and some three feet deep. This was done in October when all the leaves had fallen from the trees. The dead leaves along with other garden refuse, such as dead bedding plants and cabbage leaves, all went into the bottom of the trench. A liberal scattering of hen manure then went on top and was worked into the trench to help rot down the green material. This was all done by late October.

At that time my father followed another hobby. He was an excellent shot. My mother never knew what it was to be without something special for the weekend, with Old Joe providing us with pheasant, partridge, wild duck and many rabbit pies. If Dad ever had a bad day with the gun, you could see him slowly plodding his way up Newton Road, the reason being his gun bag was full of turnips from the farmer's field!

Dad helped to keep the vermin down for the local farmer and in return would get his manure delivered. This was the type of muck where the animals had been store fed inside the farm sheds and in early February were cleaned out. It often turned up just when all the ladies on Newton Road were cooking Sunday lunch. Mrs Miskelly, who lived next door at Number 23, always had her window open and you could smell the lunch cooking – often a strong chicken smell. Marjory at Number 19 always had a cabbage aroma wafting out of her window. The smell soon altered when Jimmy the farmer arrived with his steaming load of farmyard manure dead on twelve noon, as he was on his way for a pint at the local pub which in those days opened at Sunday lunch time.

You could hear Jimmy's tractor coming down the road but the smell of the manure preceded him and enveloped the whole of Newton Road. The ladies down the road had their little ventilator windows open to let out the steam from the boiling pans. Jimmy would reverse up onto the footpath in front of No 21 and 'slither' (that's a good Cumbrian expression) and the manure landed in a steaming heap outside the front gate.

The smell then made its way down Newton Road and you could hear the little windows being slammed. Then minutes later the dogs would come running out to investigate the new smell. After running onto the heap and rolling in it for a while, they would return home and jump on their owners' beds! We weren't very popular for about a week until Old Joe began to spread it around the back. He put some of the manure over the green material then some soil and continued to do this until he filled the trench and it looked like an elephant's grave!

"This is what you call ground preparation," he said to me. "When you put it in (meaning manure), then you can get it out (meaning fantastic crops)!" Another thing Old Joe would always say was, "How come, when you put all this smelly stuff into the trench, they come out smelling of beautiful Sweet Peas?"

I can remember all the varieties of Sweet Peas that Old Joe grew: Swan Lake, Elizabeth Taylor, Gertrude Tingay Reconnaissance, Mrs Ckay, Mrs R Bolton, Tell Tale, and Carlotta. This year I grew Swan Lake which is still an excellent Sweet Pea throwing many 'fivers' (five blooms per stem) but smaller blooms than one of the best standard whites, Royal Wedding.

My Dad won the top prize in Cumberland and Westmorland from 1950 to 1957 for the best kept and cropped allotment. I must not forget my mother though, or as I called her 'Mam'. She was a wonderful person and very caring as I remember. Every morning she would shout to get me up for work at 6.15 then 6.30 then 7.0, then 7.45! I was due at Carlton Nurseries, Joe Kerr's market garden at 8.0 – and it was four miles away. I would eventually get to my bike, which Mam had wheeled to the front of the house at about 7.45. I used to break all world records and get there at 7.59 with one minute to spare! I was totally looked after by my Mam. She would always cook wonderful meals and give me everything I ever wanted and all this was done on a meager wage from the railway.

When I was seventeen I left Penrith for agricultural college at Askham Bryan but that's another story! I never went to live back home again in Penrith on the edge of the beautiful Lake District, but when we go back I really appreciate the natural beauty of the Lakes. One of my favourite places is Ullswater, about eight miles from where I was born. Now I am lucky to live in the beautiful county of Yorkshire.

# The Lord Mayor

Over many years I have got to know a wonderful man. Not only was he a local councillor in Leeds, but he was very involved with Britain in Bloom. Frank Robinson is also an excellent speaker to clubs and horticultural societies. His topic is not politics – it is flowers and gardens he has visited all over the world. He has come three times to Leeds Horticultural Society to give us very enjoyable talks and I have had the great pleasure of making the vote of thanks.

One Sunday morning Frank and his wife visited our nursery. He had come to ask me if I would honour him at his mayor-making ceremony in Leeds Civic Hall and the reception afterwards at Leeds Town Hall. He had been given the opportunity to become Lord Mayor of Leeds. My brief was to give a short presentation during the meal and make the toast.

After talking for about eight minutes I felt Betty tugging on my jacket so that told me my time was up. I then gave the toast, which was to the Lord Mayor and Lady Mayoress, Leeds Citizens and Leeds City. I did add more – I also said Leeds United and mentioned the parks. What a wonderful occasion!

During Frank's mayoral year I was able to give a presentation in Leeds Civic Hall for the Lord Mayor's charity. One afternoon in late spring, Gordon Kirby and I arranged a Gardeners' Question Time – again for his charity.

We got a letter saying we were to receive an official visit at our nursery from the Lord Mayor and Lady Mayoress. It came on a working day but we soon closed the nursery gates. My friend Nigel was at the nursery with his log-splitting machine preparing wood for our winter fires. Nigel soon had the Lord Mayor, complete with official chain, splitting logs. We had a lovely time and Betty made afternoon tea and cakes. It was not a bad occasion for a humble gardener and his wife, and to add to it all we were presented with some  glassware with the Lord Mayor's thanks for my efforts during his year.

**Splitting logs during the visit to my nursery by the Lord Mayor and Lady Mayoress of Leeds.**

# INDEX

*Principal references are in bold.*

*2010 Titles from Great Northern Books*

ARTHRUR RANSOME – Master Storyteller – By Roger Wardale

BEATRIX POTTER – Her Lakeland Years – By W.R. Mitchell

BRONTË IN LOVE – The most tragic story Charlotte never told – By Sarah Freeman

FRITH ON CRICKET – Half a Century of Writing – By David Frith

HERRIOT – A Vet's Life – The real story of Alf Wight – By W. R. Mitchell

JOE LONGTHORNE – The Official Autobiography

LUCAS – from Soweto to Soccer Superstar – Authorised Biography of Lucas Radebe – By R Coomber

MAGNIFICENT SEVEN – Yorkshire's Championship Years 1959-69 – By Andrew Collomosse

PLAY CRICKET THE RIGHT WAY – By Geoffrey Boycott

REVIE – Revered and Reviled – By Richard Suttcliffe

THE GREAT BOOK OF YORKSHIRE PUDDING – By Elaine Lemm

THE YORKSHIRE COUNTY CRICKET CLUB YEARBOOK

*Also available from Great Northern*

BRIGHT AND BREEZY – YTV in all Weathers – By Jon Mitchell

BRIGHT DAY – By JB Priestley

DEANO – From Gipsyville to the Premiership – By Dean Windass

DELIGHT – By JB Priestley

FROM BUST TO BOOM – Hull City AFC : From the Brink of Extinction to the Premier League – By John Fieldhouse

Austin Mitchell's GRAND BOOK OF YORKSHIRE HUMOUR

HANNAH HAUXWELL – 80 years in the Dales – By W.R. Mitchell

PRIESTLEY'S WARS – By Neil Hanson

SANDMAN – The Autobiography of Cedric Robinson, Queen's Guide to the Sands

STORM FORCE – Britain's Wildest Weather – By Michael Fish, Ian McCaskill and Paul Hudson

SWEET SUMMERS – The Classic Cricket Writing of JM Kilburn – Wisden Book of the Year

THE GOOD COMPANIONS – By JB Priestley

THUNDER IN THE MOUNTAINS – The Men Who Built Ribblehead – By W.R. Mitchell

WAINWRIGHT – His Life from Milltown to Mountain – By W.R. Mitchell

WEATHERMAN – 50 years of Extreme Weather – By John Kettley

*for further information visit: www.greatnorthernbooks.co.uk*